HEGEL'S *PHENOMENOLOGY OF SPIRIT*

This book introduces Hegel's best known and most influential work, *Phenomenology of Spirit*, by interpreting it as a unified argument for a single philosophical claim: that human beings achieve their freedom through retrospective self-understanding. In clear, non-technical prose, Larry Krasnoff sets this claim in the context of the history of modern philosophy and shows how it is developed in the major sections of Hegel's text. The result is an accessible and engaging guide to one of the most complex and important works of nineteenth-century philosophy, which will be of interest to all students and teachers working in this area.

LARRY KRASNOFF is Associate Professor, Department of Philosophy, College of Charleston. He is co-editor with Natalie Brender of *New Essays on the History of Autonomy* (2004).

T0382592

CAMBRIDGE INTRODUCTIONS TO KEY PHILOSOPHICAL TEXTS

This new series offers introductory textbooks on what are considered to be the most important texts of Western philosophy. Each book guides the reader through the main themes and arguments of the work in question, while also paying attention to its historical context and its philosophical legacy. No philosophical background knowledge is assumed, and the books will be well suited to introductory university-level courses.

Titles published in the series:

DESCARTES'S *MEDITATIONS* by Catherine Wilson

WITTGENSTEIN'S *PHILOSOPHICAL INVESTIGATIONS* by David G. Stern

WITTGENSTEIN'S *TRACTATUS* by Alfred Nordmann

ARISTOTLE'S *NICOMACHEAN ETHICS* by Michael Pakaluk

SPINOZA'S *ETHICS* by Steven Nadler

KANT'S *CRITIQUE OF PURE REASON* by Jill Vance Buroker

HEIDEGGER'S *BEING AND TIME* by Paul Gorner

HEGEL'S *PHENOMENOLOGY OF SPIRIT* by Larry Krasnoff

HEGEL'S *PHENOMENOLOGY OF SPIRIT*

An Introduction

LARRY KRASNOFF

College of Charleston

CAMBRIDGE
UNIVERSITY PRESS

CAMBRIDGE
UNIVERSITY PRESS

University Printing House, Cambridge CB2 8BS, United Kingdom

Cambridge University Press is part of the University of Cambridge.

It furthers the University's mission by disseminating knowledge in the pursuit of
education, learning and research at the highest international levels of excellence.

www.cambridge.org
Information on this title: www.cambridge.org/9780521695374

First published 2008

A catalogue record for this publication is available from the British Library

Library of Congress Cataloguing in Publication data
Krasnoff, Larry, 1963–
Hegel's Phenomenology of spirit : an introduction / Larry Krasnoff.
p.   cm. – (Cambridge introductions to key philosophical texts)
Includes bibliographical references (p.   ) and index.
ISBN 978-0-521-87357-4 (hardback) – ISBN 978-0-521-69537-4 (pbk.)
1. Hegel, Georg Wilhelm Friedrich, 1770–1831. Phänomenologie des Geistes.   2. Spirit.
3. Consciousness.   4. Truth.   I. Title.   II. Series.
B2929.K73   2008
193–dc22   2007037655

ISBN 978-0-521-87357-4 Hardback
ISBN 978-0-521-69537-4 Paperback

Cambridge University Press has no responsibility for the persistence or accuracy
of URLs for external or third-party internet websites referred to in this publication,
and does not guarantee that any content on such websites is, or will remain,
accurate or appropriate.

Contents

Contents

Preface

I have long seen a need for a short introduction to Hegel's *Phenomenology of Spirit*, but at the same time I have been acutely aware that such an introduction faces severe obstacles. The first of these are immediately obvious to anyone who even thumbs through the book: the work is especially long, and it is written in a dense, abstract language that seems as if it could be comprehensible only to Hegel himself. For all of that, the work is deeply connected to themes in the history not just of philosophy but also of religion, politics, and literature, and it has been highly influential in all of those areas. One would expect that a proper introduction to any philosophical work would have at least something to say about its terminology, its particular arguments, its historical background, and its subsequent historical influences. But in this case doing justice to even one of these topics would lead to a prohibitively long book.

The situation is only partially helped by a decision to focus on a specifically philosophical introduction, by which I mean to focus specifically on what the work can be said to attempt, and to accomplish, as an argument. That sort of focus relegates the matters of historical background and influence, and even the issue of terminology, to supporting roles: the task is to convey, in clear language accessible to contemporary readers, what Hegel's main claims are meant to be. But even this particular task is complicated by the style and the diverse influences of the work, and by its sheer length. Different sorts of philosophers have different standards for what constitutes a philosophical argument, and indeed Hegel remains a kind of litmus test for this question, since the reception of his work was crucial to the still tense division between "analytic" and "Continental" philosophy. So it is virtually impossible to identify Hegel's most important arguments in a way that will satisfy every philosopher's conception of what constitutes a philosophical argument – especially when many philosophers have long thought that Hegel abandoned argumentation entirely. And there is no way to identify those most important arguments without ignoring some sections of Hegel's text, each of which is made up of dozens of sub-arguments and narrative twists. Given the length of the *Phenomenology*, this kind of introduction cannot be a commentary like one of the many already in print, the sort of book that takes itself as obligated to discuss every section of Hegel's text.[1] That sort of approach would lead, once again, to a prohibitively long book.

In navigating my way through these difficulties, I have tried to focus on the context in which an inexperienced but philosophically interested student is likely to encounter Hegel's *Phenomenology* for the first time. That context is likely to be a class for advanced undergraduates or beginning graduate students, a class that treats Hegel not on his own but in the context of a larger survey, perhaps of Kant and German idealism, but more likely of nineteenth-century or Continental philosophy. Such classes can assign only selections from the *Phenomenology* to occupy the three to four weeks that can typically be devoted to Hegel. Usually these sections come from the first parts of the work: the Preface, the Introduction, and the chapters on "Consciousness" and "Self-Consciousness." After that, there tends to be a good deal of divergence about what to read. And so my close argumentative reading of Hegel's text concentrates on the sections of the work through the chapter "Self-Consciousness" (which ends with the discussion of the Unhappy Consciousness). In this book, Chapter 5 is intended to be read alongside Hegel's Preface and Introduction, Chapter 6 is intended to be read alongside his chapter on "Consciousness," and Chapter 7 is intended to be read alongside his chapter on "Self-Consciousness." After that, in Chapter 8, I offer textual discussions only of selected sections, those that I suspect are most likely for instructors to assign. But these discussions are presented merely as excurses, which readers can feel free to either examine or ignore. In Chapters 8 and 9, I concentrate mainly on the larger question of what the later sections of the book are intended to accomplish. The idea is not just to keep the textual discussion to a manageable length, to avoid writing a 400-page commentary, but also to present the work in

---

[1] For just two recent examples, see Terry Pinkard, *Hegel's Phenomenology: The Sociality of Reason* (Cambridge University Press, 1994); and H. S. Harris, *Hegel's Ladder: A Commentary on Hegel's Phenomenology of Spirit* (Hackett, 1997). Nor, if it is to concern only the *Phenomenology*, can this be a book – like the works of Charles Taylor, Robert Pippin, and Michael Forster – that attempts to lay out Hegel's project in the *Phenomenology* and to then relate its status to the *Logic* and to Hegel's idea of a philosophical system. See Taylor, *Hegel* (Cambridge University Press, 1975); Pippin, *Hegel's Idealism: The Satisfactions of Self-Consciousness* (Cambridge University Press, 1989); and Forster, *Hegel's Idea of a Phenomenology of Spirit* (University of Chicago Press, 1998). I discuss some of these issues in Chapter 1, but only briefly.

the sort of context that professors are most likely to assign it to beginning readers.

To give focus to this study, I have also chosen to frame my discussion around a single theme: Hegel's defense of modernity as the expression and even the realization of human freedom. The historical emergence of this theme is the subject of Chapters 1 through 4. It is often pointed out that Hegel is trying to provide a new defense of modern intellectual, cultural, and social institutions, one that makes an explicit appeal to the history and development of those institutions. This kind of historical account is explicitly at odds with the traditional philosophical understanding of standards of truth and rationality as essentially timeless, and it also appeals to cultural considerations (to literature, to religion, and to political developments) that have traditionally been considered outside the boundaries of purely rational argumentation. So how is a historically grounded argument supposed to work as a philosophical justification? How can Hegel argue, as he clearly does, that he has given a full rational justification of the modern idea of freedom, and also that his account is explicitly historical?

The assumption behind this study is that Hegel's answer to these questions can be found in his distinctive account of human subjectivity, which is intended to combine the notions of freedom, rationality, and historical reflection in a very special way. On the reading I will present, the *Phenomenology* is an argument for the claim that the essential nature of subjectivity – what it is to be a human being – is to seek self-knowledge through a reflection on one's past. On this kind of view, rationality is historical because human beings come to understand themselves historically, and history is rational insofar as it tends toward institutions that affirm the value of this kind of subject, of this kind of human being. The second, substantive task of this book – which should be of interest even to those who do not need it for pedagogical purposes – is to show that the *Phenomenology of Spirit* can and should be read as a philosophical defense of these claims. On this reading, both the opening, "philosophical," chapters of the book and the subsequent "historical" chapters should be seen as part of a continuous argument for a certain view of subjectivity: not just an argument that our modern conception of subjectivity is essentially connected to culture and history, but also an argument that this historical conception of subjectivity is essentially connected to the enterprise of rational justification.

Behind all of this is the thought that a philosophical introduction to any work, Hegel's included, should not just identify but also exemplify the sort of argumentation that makes the work specifically philosophical.

That is, a philosophical introduction to Hegel should not just describe his position, but should also try to understand it as a live option in some real and ongoing philosophical debate. My hope is that by narrowing the focus of the book to a particular issue – Hegel's historical defense of his historical conception of subjectivity – the book gains in comprehensibility and philosophical focus what it necessarily lacks in comprehensiveness.² Faced with the problems posed by the length and the sprawling influences of the *Phenomenology*, I have quite deliberately abandoned the thought of a fully comprehensive introduction.³ There is much in Hegel that I will be

---

² In my discussions, I try to avoid Hegelian jargon as much as possible. As the argument unfolds, I of course try to explain what Hegel's terms mean, and to connect my own claims to specific formulations in his text. But I have not tried to provide any sort of systematic treatment of, or even introduction to, Hegel's vocabulary. This is not, therefore, a particularly good book for teaching someone to "talk" Hegel, to acquire the sort of technical facility that would, say, allow that person to open the *Logic* to a random paragraph and begin reading with fluidity and confidence. My view is that this kind of special competence is too remote and too impractical an aim for most readers of this book, and especially for students who are initially encountering Hegel for just a few weeks. The barriers posed by Hegel's terminology and writing style are so great that they demand something like the opposite approach: showing that it is possible to talk about Hegel in language accessible to any decent student of the humanities. What new (and even many old) readers of Hegel most need is the reassurance that his seemingly impenetrable formulations really do amount to claims that can be stated clearly and plausibly, and relate clearly and plausibly to familiar debates in philosophy. And they need to know that the sprawling and idiosyncratic form of the work really can be understood as serving a larger and understandable purpose. In short, my view is that in the case of Hegel, especially, a study like this one should be a lifeline of clarity dropped into what can seem like a hostile sea of obscurity: what the reader of Hegel needs to cling to, at every moment, is the thought that his work really does have a clear philosophical point. Only by believing that can the reader of Hegel believe that his philosophy is really worth reading, and that the technical competence needed to read him fluently might eventually be worth acquiring.

The emphasis on the unity and larger purpose of the work means that I will not be able to engage in any extended discussions of Hegel's contributions to particular fields of philosophy, such as epistemology or ethics, though I will have much to say that is relevant to such fields. The plan to read the text as a specifically philosophical argument will also neglect Hegel's vast influence on other areas of culture, such as history, religion, or literature; though I will again touch on matters relating to all of these, I will not be able to do anything like justice to Hegel's contributions. Together with the size, the complexity, and the intellectual range of the *Phenomenology*, these commitments mean that I will inevitably be neglecting interesting and important themes in the work. I would not claim that my particular emphasis on Hegel's conception of subjectivity as retrospective self-knowledge comes anywhere close to providing a full reading of the work. But I do believe that focusing specifically on this theme will best allow a reader to make philosophical sense of the entire work in a manageable amount of time.

³ That makes this book different from the short introductions to Hegel offered by Peter Singer or Frederick Beiser, which take themselves as obligated to discuss every important aspect of Hegel's life and work, at least very briefly, and which of necessity lose some of their philosophical focus. See Singer, *Hegel: A Very Short Introduction* (Oxford University Press, 2001); and Beiser, *Hegel* (Routledge, 2005). Beiser's account is much richer, but it is also longer and more general than what I aim for here. The book is probably closest in spirit to the shorter versions of Taylor's and Harris' books, but just because they are abridgments, it is hard to read them without feeling that one is missing something of the argument. See Taylor, *Hegel and Modern Society* (Cambridge University Press, 1975); and Harris, *Hegel: Phenomenology and System* (Hackett, 1995).

unable to discuss here: my goal is not to "cover" Hegel but rather to allow him to speak in full voice in recognizable and continuing debates over such matters as freedom, rationality, and the nature of rational justification. The results, I hope, will be a kind of clarity, a lack of clutter, and a willingness finally to listen to his position, that are sorely needed when encountering Hegel at any level.

Acknowledgments

It is always appropriately humbling to recognize how much a book owes to the work of others. At Williams College and then at Johns Hopkins University, I was fortunate to study the *Phenomenology* with a pair of gifted teachers, Mark Taylor and George Armstrong Kelly. From reading Charles Taylor, Robert Pippin, and Allen Wood, I learned a great deal more not just about Hegel, but also about how to give him a voice in the conversation of Anglo-American philosophy. When I wrote the earliest sections of this book, Edward Minar provided helpful suggestions and encouragement. Later sections were presented to audiences at Carleton College, the Northeastern Political Science Association, and the College of Charleston, and I am grateful for the responses I received on those occasions. My editor at Cambridge University Press, Hilary Gaskin, has been especially supportive and patient throughout the editorial process, and she has consistently pushed me to improve the text in ways that I otherwise would not have done. Three anonymous reviewers for the Press also provided a wide range of useful suggestions. Finally, since there is no adequate way for me to acknowledge all the support I have received from my family, I will end simply by expressing my gratitude to them.

CHAPTER I

Introduction

Let's start with a familiar historical claim, a claim that is very general, very crude, but at the same time nearly impossible to deny. The way our world looks today was decisively shaped by a series of developments that began in northern Europe some centuries ago (we can argue about exactly how many), developments that transformed northern European societies from minor or even irrelevant outposts on the fringes of Roman and Islamic civilization to the most technologically, militarily, and culturally dominant societies that the world has ever seen. The name we give to this set of developments, of course, is "modernity." Just how and when it happened is the subject of endless debate, but the debates tend to center on a series of things that happened during the sixteenth through the eighteenth centuries: the Protestant Reformation, the development of modern physics by Galileo and Newton, the exploration and conquest of the Americas, the liberalization of trade and the development of capitalist forms of exchange, the American and French Revolutions. In some combination, we can say, these developments produced a form of civilization devoted to the study and manipulation of the physical world for unapologetically material ends, in which religion is redefined as a matter of private conviction and pushed to the margins of public life, and in which politics is conceived of as grounded in democratic choice and individual human rights. The societies that conceive of the world in these ways have become so dominant that today there is a real question about whether there are any viable alternatives to these modern forms of life.

For that reason, the question of whether modernity is a good thing may seem like an irrelevant question, like asking whether oxygen is a good thing to have in our atmosphere. We may need it, but we don't have much choice in the matter. Or the developments that make up modernity may seem so general, so diffuse, and so heterogeneous that no real evaluation is possible at all. In that case, the question of whether modernity is a good thing would be more like the question of whether religion is a good thing. You can answer it, but your answer is almost certainly going to be incomplete, because religion plays so many different roles for so many different people that it doesn't amount to just one thing. Still, in a modern society, at least, everyone has to decide whether and how to be religious, and doing that will commit you to some story about what religion is and what you think it is good (or bad) for. Perhaps some of us don't have to decide whether to be modern, but we do have to decide how to relate to the parts of the world that still seem less fully modern than Europe and North America. And our decisions about that are not like our choices about religion, which we moderns might want to conceive of as affecting only ourselves. Our choices about how to relate, for example, to China, to the Middle East, or to Africa have military, political, and economic consequences that affect hundreds of millions of people. In justifying their actions, Western societies and governments are constantly telling stories about just what modernity is and what parts of it are good. Those stories might always be selective, but they are essential features of our cultural and political dialogue, and it is still true today – as it has been since the French Revolution – that the best way to understand where someone stands in the political spectrum is to understand what he or she thinks modernity is and what parts of it are good and bad.

The negative stories about modernity tend to concentrate on its economic and technological aspects: modern Western societies are devoted to capitalist exploitation, to soulless materialism, to the violent subjugation of nature or of "backward" cultures. The positive stories about modernity, on the other hand, tend to concentrate on its moral and political aspects and, in particular, on the notion of human freedom. In one form or another, the various positive stories about modernity tend to come down to some form of the following claim: whereas once human beings were seen as bound by class, by religion, or by cultural tradition to a fixed station in life, now modern human beings are understood as essentially free. They are free to worship according to their own convictions, free to pursue material happiness as far as their abilities can take them, free to select their own rulers, and free to choose or to abandon a particular way of life. Many or even most of these positive stories of modern freedom are crude and unconvincing: they discount or dismiss the extent to which the supposedly free choices of modern individuals are constrained by economic, technological, and cultural forces far beyond any individual's control. But since this narrative of freedom still occupies a central place in our moral and political dialogue, it cannot be dismissed until it has been studied in its most influential and sophisticated forms.

Of course influence and sophistication are two very different things, but there are rare cases in which they are combined, and the case of the

Phenomenology of Spirit happens to be one of those. If you are reading the *Phenomenology* for the first time, you should and almost certainly will be asking yourself what the point of reading this book is, particularly when the book is so long, so dense, so abstract, so idiosyncratic in its language, and so blithely uncompromising about all of those things that it can seem like the product of monumental self-absorption or the observations of some visitor from an alien galaxy. With a famous and famously difficult book like the *Phenomenology*, there are always many possible answers to that question; the book always has and always will be interpreted in many different ways. But the answer I will argue for here is just this one: there is probably no more influential and no more sophisticated presentation of the narrative of modern freedom than what Hegel offers in this book.

On the one hand, it remains true even in contemporary debates that to stake a claim to the positive narrative of modern freedom is just to count as a kind of Hegelian. To claim that the modern world represents a kind of progress toward the realization of human freedom is to make the sort of sweeping historical generalization that is often simply dismissed as "Hegelian." On the other hand, a Hegelian in contemporary debates is also someone who is sensitive to the criticism that the freely choosing individual of the optimistic account of modernity is too isolated from historical and cultural reality to be anything other than an illusion. Although he championed modernity as in some sense nothing more than the individual's coming to understand and value his or her own freedom, Hegel also deployed most if not all of the criticisms that have been subsequently leveled at the modern notion of freedom. On Hegel's account, the idea of freedom is not simply a property of the individual's will but also a cultural achievement, one that emerged through a long process of historical development. That process of development, restated in a unique and highly abstract form – a form that Hegel understood as appropriately philosophical but that subsequent generations of readers have understood as everything from seductively literary to repugnantly verbose – is what is described in the *Phenomenology of Spirit*.

HEGEL'S LIFE AND WORK

What first drew Hegel himself to the narrative of modern freedom was, it seems, the French Revolution. Georg Wilhelm Friedrich Hegel was born in 1770, the son of a low-level civil servant from Stuttgart.[1] He was a talented student, and so at the age of eighteen, he was sent off in the traditional

---

[1] An impressive recent biographical account of Hegel's life and work in English is Terry Pinkard, *Hegel: A Biography* (Cambridge University Press, 2000).

direction for intellectually gifted young men. In 1788, he entered the semi-
nary at the University of Tübingen. There he met and became close friends
with two of his fellow students, Friedrich Schelling and Friedrich Hölderlin.
From this friendship emerged, over the next few decades, some of the most
important contributions to the intellectual life of Germany. Schelling would
go on to become a well-known idealist philosopher, until Hegel himself
far eclipsed him in that role. As for Hölderlin, he would become one of
the most celebrated of all German poets. In the early 1790s, however, they
were just struggling students, ostensibly preparing for careers as Lutheran
ministers. But the Revolution seems to have interrupted their plans. As
undergraduates, the young Hegel, Schelling, and Hölderlin decided they
had a more important job to do, which was to assist in the birth of a new
and better world.

On the face of it, theirs was an unpromising location for the work of
revolution. No matter how fast events were unfolding in Paris, they had
little effect on the dreary politics of southwestern Germany. The medieval
University of Tübingen was a locally prestigious place to study for the
ministry, but in the 1790s it was not even a backwater of the Enlightenment.
Its faculty were doctrinally conservative and unlikely even to have read
Rousseau. Hegel, Schelling, and Hölderlin read him, of course, but then
they were faced with the problem of applying this most modern of thinkers
to a German reality that seemed very far from modern. In England, France,
and the United States, freedom now seemed to be a political reality. But the
Germans were just starting to talk about the Rights of Man, and even doing
that could get you into trouble with the local authorities. And it was not as
if the various German monarchies had much to show for themselves in the
way of military or economic power. In every respect, Germany seemed to
be well behind the rest of Europe. But Hegel and his friends inherited and
then expanded an intellectual context that managed to put the problem of
German backwardness to creative and productive use. Two sources were
crucial for this intellectual context: first, the philosophy of Immanuel Kant,
and second, the development of German Romanticism.

For all the later German idealists, Hegel included, Kant was first and
foremost a theorist of human freedom. It is the autonomous agent of Kant's
practical philosophy that earned him the title of the philosopher of the
French Revolution. But Kant's special contribution came in turning the
modern notion of freedom into a specifically philosophical problem. I will
discuss this problem extensively in Chapters 3 and 4, but for now it is enough
to say that while the modern world and its revolutions were proclaiming the
freedom of all human beings, Kant insisted that the more important tasks

were to understand the nature of this freedom and its place in a modern view of the world. Just what entitled human beings to say that they really are free? And since this kind of question was theoretical or philosophical in nature, it could be studied – and perhaps even better studied – from the politically irrelevant safety of a Königsberg or a Tübingen. In a late essay on the French Revolution, Kant himself went on to make an even more extreme version of the point: the real sign of historical progress was not anything that happened in Paris, but rather the enthusiastic responses of the rest of Europe to the revolutionary events.[2] Only the "disinterestedness" of these "spectators" – their inability even to consider acting within their benighted monarchies – could assure a morally pure motive for their approval, and only a morally pure motive could guarantee the goodness of the historical phenomenon that was being judged. On this view, the task of historical progress required a kind of international division of labor: it was the French and perhaps the Americans who would act, but it was the Germans who would comprehend, theorize, and finally justify those actions.

Kant's focus on the theoretical problem of freedom had an especially important consequence for his German idealist successors. The natural starting point for thinking about this problem is the nature of a free agent who, as free, is understood as independent of external determination. This starting point is what drives what is still the most familiar and influential criticism of Kant: that he presupposes an abstract, isolated, and unappealing conception of human beings as purely free and rational. These free and rational beings, it is alleged, are radically cut off from others, from society and culture, and even from their own biological natures. In the context of later German idealism, the specific response to this kind of criticism was a specifically German form of Romanticism.

Taken broadly and hence very crudely, Romanticism is a response to the Enlightenment's emphasis on rationality, a response that celebrates the powers of emotion and imagination. This response is often described as a critique of the Enlightenment, but a better description would be a kind of adaptation to the limits that the Enlightenment places on the public expression of religious faith. If religion has no role to play in the scientific description of the world, or in political life, then it can only find expression in the private realm of faith and individual conscience. The result, the defining feature of Romanticism, is an intense spiritualization of

---

[2] Kant, "An Old Question Raised Again: Is The Human Race Continually Progressing?" (Part II of *The Conflict of Faculties*, 1798), in *On History*, ed. Lewis White Beck (Prentice Hall, 1963), pp. 144–159. For a sympathetic reading of the argument of this essay, see my "The Fact of Politics: History and Teleology in Kant," *European Journal of Philosophy* 2(1), pp. 22–40.

inner experience as a source of power and meaning. This sacralization of inwardness necessarily implies a turning away from the everyday world of social interaction, which always appears as pallid and even oppressive, as a disregard for the force of inner truth. In Britain and later in America, in the more "advanced" modern countries, this turning away from social life tended to imply a turning away from political questions. But in a less politically modern context, like that of Germany, it was still possible to reject the current political reality while defending Enlightenment politics. The English Romantics and the American Transcendentalists, who already had forms of democratic politics, found them mostly boring and dispiriting, and looked within for a more radical kind of human freedom. But their German Romantic counterparts, who were yet to experience democracy, were able to combine their cravings for inner significance with their desires for political freedom. Since both were remote enough from their own lived experience, they were able to imagine their common fulfillment in a different sort of society, one with an intense (and hence appropriately spiritualized) commitment to democratic values (and hence appropriately committed to equality).[3]

The favorite German Romantic candidate for this imagined society was classical Athenian democracy, sometimes linked with the pre-Christian and hence pagan German tribal past. Again, the contrast with English and later American Romanticism is instructive here. To the extent that English-speaking Romantics did think politically, they looked forward, proposing new, utopian communities whose values would be even more "advanced" than those of electoral democracies. German Romantics, by contrast, tended to look backward, to the Greek and Teutonic past. The claim that German Romanticism could achieve an even more advanced version of democratic politics would have been impossible to sustain in the German political reality of the 1790s (or even the 1840s). Instead the German Romantics needed to establish that they had any claim to democratic values, and they attempted to do that by looking backward past their petty monarchs to a deeper, classical past.

The result of all of this was a particular Romantic vision that gripped Hegel and his young friends in the 1790s, the early and enthusiastic years

---

[3] For an extensive treatment of the intellectual context of German Romanticism, see Frederick Beiser, *Enlightenment, Revolution and Romanticism: The Genesis of Modern German Political Thought, 1790–1800* (Harvard University Press, 1992); and *The Romantic Imperative: The Concept of Early German Romanticism* (Harvard University Press, 2004).

of German idealism. That vision was of a spiritualized community of free beings, united together not by political coercion or economic interest but by a shared culture of art and poetry that celebrated the freedom of the individual. The emphases on culture and emotion were intended as correctives to the excessive rationality and abstraction of Kant's positions, and also served as useful substitutes for the dubious political institutions of the various German monarchies. If the worry suggested by both Kant's philosophy and local German politics was that the modern idea of freedom might be nothing more than a mere idea, then the German Romantics responded that it was an especially sublime idea, one that was worthy of celebration in artistic and religious terms, and that would unite human beings as never before – except perhaps in the most wonderful of cultures, that of ancient Greeks. To say that this vision stood in sharp contrast to the reality of the Tübingen of the 1790s was not any sort of criticism. The sharp contrast was the whole point.

Among his group of young friends, Hegel was always the sober "old man," and his distance from their enthusiasm only increased over time. There are passages in Hegel's early philosophical works, and in the *Phenomenology* itself, that share the tone of grandiose but still earnest piety that is characteristic of Fichte and Hölderlin, but they are quickly muted by Hegel's far deeper enthusiasm for theoretical abstraction. It did not take long for Hegel to realize that his intellectual talents were better suited to an academic than a pastoral or a literary career. After graduating from the University of Tübingen, he worked first as a private tutor in Berne and in Frankfurt, and then as a *Privatdozent* (an unsalaried lecturer, paid by individual students who chose to take his classes) at the University of Jena. His first published philosophical works, *The Difference between Fichte's and Schelling's Systems of Philosophy* and *Faith and Knowledge*, are primarily works in theoretical philosophy, concerned with the possibility of knowledge rather than the celebration of human freedom. But even in these works, Hegel is concerned with defending a version of the ecstatic vision of the German Romantics: the union of the free subject with a larger world in which it now finds itself to be at home (to know and to act in). The question that Hegel's mature philosophy takes up with increasing focus is how this vision of unity can be something more than a fervent hope, how it can be defended not with emotional appeals but with rational arguments.

In his mature work, Hegel's way of characterizing the achievement of this unity is to speak of Spirit's coming to know, or to realize, itself. The term *Spirit* (*Geist*) of course raises special problems, and I will take up some of the most important of these in Chapter 5.[4] For now, what we need to understand is that Spirit is intended to refer both to historically and culturally authoritative standards and practices, as well as to the nature of subjectivity itself. What Spirit really is, for Hegel, is a kind of collective and historical subject, which expresses the nature of freedom in cultural and historical practices. The full maturity or self-development of Spirit – and this is the odd way that Hegel likes to talk – would also represent the realization of the modern idea of freedom, the unity of Kant's abstract and purely rational idea of freedom with the cultural, social, and political practices that would embody and sustain it.

Hegel's life project, on which he worked as the rector of a gymnasium in Nürnberg, as a professor at the University of Heidelberg, and then until his death in 1831, at the University of Berlin, was the construction of what he called a philosophical system. Within this system, everything would have rational justification, which in Hegel's terms means deriving from the process of Spirit's self-realization. In a sense, what Hegel tried to do was to identify the rational core of nearly every area of human thought (logic, science, morality, politics, aesthetics, religion, and history) by describing them as part of Spirit's self-expression in history, as part of a sprawling story that describes a path toward the realization of human freedom in the modern world. In the synoptic presentation offered in his *Encyclopedia of the Philosophical Sciences* (1817, revised editions in 1827 and 1830), Hegel lays out this philosophical system in three stages: a Philosophy of Nature

---

[4] Hegel's usage is highly idiosyncratic, and to avoid misunderstanding or simply dismissing it, we need to consider the various meanings that Hegel wants to link together in this one term. The idea of Spirit is meant to include all of the following:

(1) those aspects of humanity which distinguish us from the rest of physical nature and which are specifically concerned with our conscious mental life (the realm of the "spiritual")

(2) the norms and practices that our culture takes to be authoritative (the usage that survives in the phrase – itself inspired by Hegel – "the spirit of the age")

(3) God, or at least the aspect of the divine that, in Christian doctrine, is supposed to indicate the presence of the heavenly God in the earthly realm (the Holy Spirit)

It may seem that both (1) and (3) require some sort of metaphysical commitment, a claim that there exists a reality that goes beyond the material. A significant amount of recent scholarship, however, both in German and in English, tries to understand and often to defend Hegel's arguments without assuming metaphysical claims. (See the discussion in note 6.) Not surprisingly, that means emphasizing (2) over (1) and (3), which raises the question of why Hegel or anyone else would bother speaking of an entity called Spirit as opposed to cultural norms or practices. But Hegel's position is that the authority of rationally justified norms and practices comes from their relation to the essential nature of human subjectivity as retrospective self-understanding. This claim does imply that certain norms have a special sort of authority to command us (a crucial part of what is implied in [3]) and that this authority comes from our retrospective self-understanding (a capacity which physical objects and lower animals do not have, which is a version of [1]).

and a Philosophy of Spirit, preceded by an introductory section called the Logic.[5] This organization is modeled on Kant's attempt to present the rational norms of belief and then of action in a two-part philosophical doctrine consisting of a metaphysics of nature and a metaphysics of morals, preceded by a "critical" analysis (originally just the *Critique of Pure Reason* but later expanded to include all three *Critiques*) of the possibility of making metaphysical claims. In Hegel's version, the *Logic* is meant to ground the Philosophies of Nature and of Spirit by showing that any judgment, any claim of a believing or acting agent, somehow implies a reference to Spirit's self-realization.

In the systematic account presented in the *Encyclopedia*, the subject of the *Phenomenology of Spirit*— consciousness – is just one of three divisions of the section on "subjective Spirit," which is itself just one of the three divisions of the Philosophy of Spirit. Beyond "subjective Spirit" lies "objective Spirit" (discussed more extensively in the *Philosophy of Right* of 1821, Hegel's main work in moral and political philosophy, and in his *Philosophy of History*, published after Hegel's death from students' notes) and "absolute Spirit" (discussed more extensively in the lectures on aesthetics, religion, and the history of philosophy, also posthumously published from notes). In that sense, the project of the *Phenomenology* would seem to constitute a small and not particularly central piece of Hegel's philosophy, which would seem to depend most critically on the success of the *Logic*. Nonetheless the *Phenomenology* has always been the most influential of Hegel's works.

Some of the reasons for this influence are stylistic. The *Phenomenology* is still a relatively early work, published in 1807, before Hegel's academic reputation and career were fully secure. Finished as Napoleon's troops were descending upon Jena, the book retains some of the German Romantic expectation of a better but still uncertain future rather than the later Hegel's synoptic, Olympian pronouncements on the completed past. It has a literary flourish that the more systematic works lack: the book has the structure of a kind of novel, in which Spirit embarks on a biographical journey from naïveté to maturity. The attempt to turn highly abstract concepts into literary characters produces writing that is often lugubrious and sometimes even laughable, but there are a good many sustained passages in which Hegel's writing achieves a genuine narrative power, in which the theoretical debates of the past take on a dramatic form that is very different from the descriptions offered by more typical philosophical works.

---

[5] The "Encyclopedia Logic" is a shortened version of Hegel's larger *Science of Logic*, which was published in three stages from 1812 to 1816.

Even for those who discarded Hegel's terminology and philosophical aspirations, something of this style has animated much subsequent cultural and intellectual history.

But the book's influence has philosophical roots as well. Although the organization of the *Encyclopedia* suggests that the study of the way Spirit appears to consciousness is just of one of Spirit's many forms, this study plays an especially important role in the justification of Hegel's philosophical claims. To study the way Spirit appears to consciousness is to study the path that thought takes to get to the idea of Spirit, which for Hegel means the path that thought takes to get to a properly philosophical perspective. Hence the *Phenomenology* is conceived as a kind of preliminary work, an introduction to Hegel's philosophical system. Since Hegel conceives of a philosophical system as complete in itself, needing no external support, the introduction to his system must ultimately be a part of the system itself. The introduction is really a kind of justification of the system, a way of showing those outside the system – or, more precisely, those who might take themselves to be outside it – the need for the system in the first place. That is, the work is a defense of the idea of Spirit for those who might think they could do without it. It traces the path from non-philosophical to philosophical thinking, a path that turns out to be the journey of Spirit itself. The *Phenomenology* is, like all of Hegel's mature philosophical works, a kind of history of Spirit, but it is a history that seeks to derive the philosophical perspective of Spirit's self-development from a starting point that does without this perspective. For those who are skeptical of Hegel's attempt to justify the modern notion of freedom by understanding it as the historical process of Spirit's self-realization, the *Phenomenology* is the crucial text to read, because this skeptical perspective is exactly the one assumed in the text itself.

HISTORY AND JUSTIFICATION

So far I have said virtually nothing about what "Spirit's self-realization" could really mean, other than to suggest that it has something to do with the historical and cultural development of the modern idea of freedom, and with what Hegel understands as a properly philosophical perspective. But even these vague suggestions immediately raise a problem, one that will be at the center of this study. How can Hegel combine his emphasis on history with a philosophical emphasis on rational justification? It seems clear that Hegel wants to offer some sort of historically sensitive defense of the modern notion of freedom, and to offer a defense is obviously to offer some sort of justification. But if the defense is to be historically sensitive, it would seem to apply only historically – that is, only to the cultures and societies that have had the relevant history. That would appear to weaken the sort of justification available for modern freedom, and thus to weaken the sort of claims that could be made on behalf of Western cultures and governments in relation to non-Western societies. In contemporary debates, Hegel is often understood in just this way: he is seen as a kind of communitarian, and thus as someone who might be sympathetic to the view that the narrative of modern freedom threatens to impose alien values on other cultures. This understanding is sharply at odds with the actual beliefs of the historical Hegel, who was an unabashed champion of modern freedom as a source for global and not just local progress. But despite Hegel's historicist commitments, this understanding is also at odds with Hegel's deeper theoretical commitments, with the "philosophical Hegel." For Hegel did not think he had in any sense weakened or restricted the justificatory power of his argument by making it historical. Instead he thought he had strengthened it and, for the first time, achieved the kind of final justification to which Western philosophers since Socrates had aspired. So the problem for us becomes trying to understand how Hegel's defense of freedom could be intended as both historically sensitive and fully justifying.

Again, if the defense is to be historical, it remains the case that the account of freedom will be justified only to those who have had the relevant history. Still, what it means to have a relevant history is not a simple matter of historical fact. No one would say that the American Revolution is not relevant to contemporary Americans' history simply because no contemporary Americans, nor even many of their ancestors, were present in 1776. What it means for the Revolution to be a part of Americans' history is that some sort of narrative that includes it is somehow important for them, for understanding who they are. What Hegel wants to say is that by writing the sort of philosophical history he has, he has made the narrative of modern freedom crucial for all of us, no matter who we are. In that sense, what Hegel has to do in his historical narrative is to convince us that his account of freedom implies a problem that everyone somehow has, and that only Hegel's account is able to solve. What the *Phenomenology* has to convince us of is that we are all the sort of free agents described in the narrative of modern freedom, and that we will not understand ourselves or our freedom until we understand that narrative.

In this study, I will argue that we can best understand Hegel's argument for these claims about freedom if we see him for a particular account of what it means to be a human being. The truth of this account is meant to be universal, not historically relative, although Hegel also claims, crucially, that we can come to understand and accept the truth of the account only under certain historical conditions, namely those that prevail in the modern world.

The account begins with three interrelated claims. First, Hegel holds that it is essential to our identities that we can only understand who we are by a process of reflection on our past experiences, on our own histories. Second, Hegel holds that any such process of reflection will involve a consideration of the larger social, cultural, and historical forces that shaped our individual development. Third, Hegel holds that this reflective process, to count as reflective, will also involve the individual's endorsing (and hence perhaps rejecting) particular social, cultural, and historical practices or norms as his or her own. These claims, Hegel believes, are simply consequences of our being reflective individuals who come to maturity within human culture.

Together, argues Hegel, the claims imply a problem about how to reconcile our independent identities as reflective agents with our inevitable determination by social, cultural, and historical forces. Because conformity to social practice or tradition is, in itself, no satisfying answer to the question of what sort of person we want to be, we need to appeal to some deeper standard of justification. The traditional aspiration of Western philosophy has been to find some fully rational standard of justification, one that would be independent of time and place, of culture and history. Now the crucial historical feature of Hegel's argument is that the difficulty of finding such a standard has become especially acute in modernity, and that modern Western societies are precisely the ones that have become conscious of the problem in an explicit way. Indeed, Hegel's argument is that the development of this self-consciousness just *is* the modern narrative of freedom. That narrative is relevant to everyone, then, because it is simply the explicit self-consciousness of a problem that confronts any reflective agent.

That there is a deep connection between the modern narrative of freedom and this philosophical problem of justification is already a complicated and controversial claim, one that will require Hegel to provide a great deal of historical argument. But it would seem that nothing in such an argument would provide any sort of solution to the philosophical problem. That modernity raises a crucial philosophical question does not mean that modernity is able to answer it. But Hegel also believes that modernity does provide the solution; indeed, his claim is that the modern self-consciousness about the problem, rightly conceived, is already the solution to the problem. As we have already noted, Hegel's own official way of putting this point is to say: the modern world is Spirit's coming to know itself.

That kind of sentence, of course, is the reason why commentaries were invented. In this commentary, I will argue that Hegel's sentence should be read in the following way: what it means for us to be modern, free individuals is to understand and endorse our identities as people who emerged from a certain process of historical development, namely one in which modern individuals came finally to accept their relation to history and culture in the first place. What I will argue is that Hegel's version of the modern narrative of freedom is a philosophical argument for a particular conception of human beings: as essentially committed to a kind of retrospective understanding of their own historical development and, in particular, to a retrospective self-understanding of the modern world. Throughout the book, I will continually speak of Hegel as defending a particular conception of human subjectivity: as retrospective self-understanding. What "Spirit's coming to know itself" means, I want to say, is that in the modern world, our nature as retrospective self-knowers is finally accepted and thereby achieved.

This book thus seeks to make basic philosophical sense of the *Phenomenology* by reading it as a unified argument for this particular conception of subjectivity.[6] The goal is to take what I take to be the central sections and

---

[6] Those familiar with Hegel scholarship will likely want to know how the reading offered here fits into that scholarship. There is no way a book like this one could ever do justice to the wealth of scholarly commentary on Hegel, but I do think it can make a contribution, particularly to debates about the kind of justification that Hegel can claim for his arguments. This is an issue that, even in the best writing on Hegel, has too often been obscured.

For a long time, it was assumed that Hegel's thought depended on a metaphysical appeal to a special sort of divine substance that nonetheless pervaded the material world; even for Anglo-American philosophers sympathetic to Continental philosophy, this ontological talk of *Geist* seemed pre-modern and dogmatic. So it was common to find Anglo-American writers on Hegel suggesting that while he had some outlandish and outdated things to say about Science, Spirit, and Absolute Knowledge, he did have some interesting and important things to say about culture, history, and politics. This sort of view, common to writers as different as Charles Taylor and Richard Rorty, makes Hegel into a somewhat crazed Romantic pantheist who nonetheless happened upon some insightful interpretations of Western culture. See Taylor, *Hegel and Modern Society* (Cambridge University Press, 1979), especially pp. 66–72; and Rorty, "Nineteenth Century Idealism and Twentieth Century Textualism," in *Consequences of Pragmatism* (University of Minnesota Press, 1980), pp. 139–159. But on this sort of reading, Hegel's thought that he arrived at these interpretations after a systematic reflection on the efforts of his philosophical predecessors becomes, at best, quaint; indeed it is hard to see why Hegel should count as a philosopher at all.

In response, a more recent vein of scholarship has tried to reinterpret Hegel in explicitly anti-metaphysical and even naturalistic terms, essentially making Hegelianism safe for contemporary philosophy. This scholarship, best represented in English by the work of Robert Pippin, has returned squarely to Hegel's main philosophical works, including the *Phenomenology*, and has made the case for Hegel as a philosopher mainly by reading him as a kind of radicalized Kantian. See Pippin, *Hegel's Idealism: The Satisfactions of Self-Consciousness* (Cambridge University Press, 1989). For the big-picture story of modern European philosophy into which Pippin intends his account of Hegel to fit, see his quite accessible *Modernism as a Philosophical Problem* (Blackwell, 1991 and 1999).

the central arguments of Hegel's work, and to explain them in a way that relates them to a single philosophical project, one that can be understood as driving both the form and the content of the entire book.

For two other recent analytic treatments of Hegel which can be usefully compared with Pippin's, see Terry Pinkard, *Hegel's Phenomenology: The Sociality of Reason* (Cambridge University Press, 1994); and Michael Forster, *Hegel's Idea of a Phenomenology of Spirit* (University of Chicago Press, 1998).

Specifically, Pippin has argued that Hegel should be understood not simply as asking an essentially Kantian question – under what conditions can we say that our judgments count as rational? – but also as answering that question in an essentially Kantian way – when those judgments come not directly from experience or from a metaphysical reality, but rather when they are guided by standards that we have imposed on ourselves as governing legitimate claims to knowledge or to rightness (*Hegel's Idealism*, pp. 3–15; *Modernism as a Philosophical Problem*, pp. 65–68). Then the question becomes: what are those self-imposed standards? And here Pippin understands Hegel as arguing, against Kant, that there are no pure or formal standards of rationality, given by reason to itself; rather, the rational standards we have are those that have emerged in the dialectical contest of views that constitutes the history and development of modern social and cultural institutions (*Modernism as a Philosophical Problem*, pp. 70–71). On this sort of reading, Hegel's claim that *Geist* pervades all things is not an attempt to find the divine in nature, but rather an attempt to show that rational judgments cannot be understood as rational without an appeal to the history and development of modern standards of judgment.

I have learned a great deal from this body of work, and there is much in the subsequent chapters that is deeply indebted to it. But as these last formulations should suggest, while commentators like Pippin, Pinkard, and Forster have succeeded in grappling with Hegel's philosophical claims as well as with his historical and cultural analyses, they have mainly seen the philosophical claims as legitimating the historical and cultural analyses and not (also) the other way around. That is, they have basically read Hegel as providing a philosophical argument for a historicist account of knowledge, and then taken his historical analyses as potential contributions to historicist accounts of particular cultural phenomena. In so doing, they have pushed to the side Hegel's view that his historical analyses are intended to complete his philosophical project, to justify his philosophical claims and not simply to follow them. And that means that Hegel's claims to full justification are also pushed to the side. If modern social and cultural institutions are to be given a full justification, it is not enough to say that standards of rationality are historically conditioned, and then to say that modern social and cultural institutions are those that have emerged from our particular historical experience. Hegel is saying that they have emerged from such a historical experience, but he is also saying that they have a trans-historical claim to rationality that legitimates them in a rather deep way. It is not just that rationality is somehow historical; it is also that a certain sort of history can be shown to be rational. It is this last claim – and, in general, Hegel's claims about the nature of history and historical progress – that recent Anglophone commentary has tended to ignore. For a very stark rejection of this part of Hegel's view, see Forster, *Hegel's Idea of a Phenomenology of Spirit*, pp. 291–295. For Pippin's similar discomfort, see *Modernism as a Philosophical Problem*, pp. 73–77.

The notorious Hegelian view that we are trying to understand here is that in the modern period, *Geist* somehow comes to know itself. On the naturalist reading of interpreters like Pippin and Pinkard, *Geist* has tended to mean not a distinct kind of metaphysical substance but merely a community's self-understanding of its most privileged norms. But if *Geist* is already self-understanding, then the notion of *Geist*'s self-understanding threatens to become a kind of tautology, reducing the thought that history is *Geist*'s coming to know itself to an essentially empty claim. Pinkard's account is instructive here: he is far less dismissive of Hegel's historical teleology, and he has a nice opening discussion of the issues in *Hegel's Phenomenology*, pp. 3–17, especially pp. 11–13. But on Pinkard's own formulation, the *Phenomenology* amounts to an account of what "the modern European community" has come to regard as rational justification (p. 13), and as he himself admits at the end of his book (pp. 334–335), this is insufficient for the sort of full justification to which Hegel aspires. On Pinkard's

PLAN OF THE WORK

I will begin by situating Hegel's retrospective account of subjectivity against the background of the history of modern philosophy. My goal here is simply to motivate Hegel's argument in the *Phenomenology*, and so especially confident readers who want to plunge directly into that argument could jump immediately to the textual discussion that begins in Chapter 5. But I presume that most readers will need and want more in the way of background. In particular, much more needs to be said about the connection between the modern conception of freedom and the traditional philosophical project of rational justification, and about how Hegel's account of subjectivity is supposed to respond to both. So I plan to spend the next three chapters discussing how these themes emerge from the history of modern philosophy. Chapter 2 concentrates on issues in epistemology and metaphysics, while Chapter 3 turns to issues in moral and political philosophy. I argue, however, that these seemingly distinct conversations in early modern philosophy ultimately converge on a common problem, one that emerges with particular force from the work of Hume and Rousseau, and that all the German idealists, from Kant through Hegel, are trying to solve. So, at least, I will argue in Chapter 4.

We have already mentioned a version of that problem in our discussion of a historically sensitive justification of the idea of freedom. That our idea of freedom might be historically specific is just one possible consequence of a more general assumption (realization?) that all of these Enlightenment and post-Enlightenment philosophers take to be distinctively modern. The

view, though, this problem is to be addressed by a shift from merely European to "world" history. This is correct as far as it goes, but it is also true that what ultimately justifies the Hegelian account of world history is its connection to the idea of a subject and its coming to self-consciousness – and it is this idea that is defended in the *Phenomenology*. So once again the sense in which Hegel's historical arguments are supposed to complete the project of philosophical justification is obscured.

We can of course say that what distinguishes the modern period in history is that we are aware that our communal self-understandings are nothing more than self-understandings, that they cannot be grounded in an independent metaphysical reality. But this is not yet to say why this kind of self-consciousness about our modern self-understandings should constitute a general justification for those particular modern self-understandings. What is so special about this kind of self-consciousness, and how can it count as a justification of modern social and cultural institutions? The issue here concerns not just the contingent historical features of modern life, but also the way those historical features reflect some sort of rationally privileged self-understanding. The deep questions being raised here are: just what is this self-understanding, and what gives it such a special privilege? As I suggested in the Preface, the reading offered here will claim that the relevant self-understanding is human beings' sense of ourselves as essentially subjects who seek self-knowledge through a reflection on our pasts. On this kind of view, rationality is historical because human beings come to understand themselves historically, and history is rational insofar as it tends toward institutions that affirm the value of this kind of subject, of this kind of human being.

modern assumption is just this: that the concepts we use to describe the world are not given to us by God or by nature; rather, our concepts are specifically human constructions, and as such, they carry no special warrant that makes them particularly suited to comprehend the nature of reality. In one way, this view is simply a radicalization of the nominalism that entered late medieval philosophy in the work of Ockham, and that strongly influenced the empiricist tradition from Hobbes through Hume. But before Hume, the empiricist tradition also clings to a hope that the concepts we invent to describe the world might be purified in a way that gives us a kind of direct access to nature. As I will argue in the next two chapters, Hume abandons any such hope, even as he remains deeply committed to a form of naturalism. Without the possibility of a purely natural language, nominalism becomes the view that our concepts are simply human conventions, and then the question is how to show that some particular set of human conventions could have rational justification, without resorting to the view that we have direct access to God or to nature, to reality as it is itself. In the account I will present here, German idealism is the Western philosophical tradition's most sustained attempt to solve this problem, by connecting the nature of rational justification to the nature of human freedom. For all of the German idealists, from Kant to Hegel, to be free means not to be bound to any external constraints, whether those constraints are said to come from nature or from God. And to be rational, in the idealists' novel account, is to bind oneself to only those constraints that we can endorse as consistent with our freedom.

On this view, the idea of freedom suggests both modernity's skepticism about justification (we are no longer certain that there are any standards that we must accept as conforming to the essential nature of reality) and the modern answer to that skepticism (we should endorse as rational just those standards that reflect our commitment to our nature as free beings). The modern narrative of freedom, for the German idealists, is crucial because it reflects a deep problem about rational justification (how to show that any standards of belief or conduct are justified) that arises with special force under modern conditions (we are no longer confident that we have divine or natural access to such standards). The problem then becomes to describe the nature of our freedom, and to show that it somehow implies a commitment to norms of belief and of action that we can take to be rationally justified. Kant's is the most influential attempt to pose and then to solve this problem, but it is Hegel's view that only his account of retrospective subjectivity can overcome the limitations of the Kantian account.

This emphasis on freedom would seem to suggest a focus on issues in moral and political philosophy, and indeed I think that practical philosophy has a certain priority for all the German idealists. But I also think that practical philosophy has this priority precisely because the German idealists believe that the idea of freedom is crucial to rational justification taken generally, to explaining the rational authority of our concepts in both the theoretical and practical realms. The authority of both modern science and modern politics depends, for both Kant and Hegel, on our showing that the norms that support these practices derive from the nature of human beings as essentially free. This, I will now argue, is the lesson to be learned from the history of early modern philosophy.

CHAPTER 2

Knowledge

It is often said that the main task of early modern philosophy is the epistemological project of showing how knowledge is possible, of explaining how
we as subjects can know the true nature of objects. At some general level,
this formulation is almost certainly right. But there are ways of explaining this epistemological project that are more misleading than helpful. For
instance, a familiar way of talking about early modern accounts of knowledge, especially in the context of survey courses that run from Descartes
to Kant, is to emphasize the problem of the external world. According to
this familiar narrative, the epistemological problem of early modern philosophy is to show how a conscious subject is entitled to infer that his or
her own individual sensations and thoughts can amount to knowledge of
an external world of objects.

Once the problem is posed in this form, it appears that the only solution
is some sort of idealism, some claim to the effect that what we even mean
by a physical object depends on the contribution of a subject. The bluntest
version of this claim, of course, was that proposed by Berkeley: a material
object is just a particular collection of ideas in our minds. On this view,
to see a tree is just to have certain ideas in our minds, and as for why it
is that you and I both seem to have the same ideas placed in our minds
when we observe and discuss the tree, Berkeley appeals to the power and
goodness of God, who causes these ideas to appear to us simultaneously,
making a shared account of nature possible.[1] If the continual intervention
of the divine will seems like an unpromising basis for the objectivity of
physical science, we can turn instead to what has often been taken to be
Kant's version of idealism, on which a physical object is the combined
result of our own mental activity and the causality of things as they are in
themselves, which, since they lie outside the workings of our own minds,
are entirely unknowable by us. If the workings of noumenal causality seem

---

[1] George Berkeley, *A Treatise Concerning the Principles of Human Knowledge*, Part I, 1–24, 30–33, 58–63.

too mysterious to admit into our account of knowledge, then we can at least understand that Kant found them just as mysterious himself, and so we can see Kant's idealism as admirably instructive in rigorously failing to find what early modern philosophy was looking for. If the modern epistemological problem is to show how our sensations can be said to be sensations of a real world of independent objects, then Kant's contribution to modern philosophy was to show that this problem is insoluble, by arguing that, as Strawson famously wrote, "reality is supersensible and we can have no knowledge of it."[2]

It is not surprising that the usual lesson that is drawn from this narrative is that the epistemological project of early modern philosophy is a dead end. But while we can agree that a view that describes human beings as disembodied subjects who exist only in their own thoughts seems unappealing in almost every way, making that picture central to early modern philosophy makes it rather puzzling why it was ever of intellectual interest to anyone, including the early modern philosophers themselves. But in fact this way of looking at the period gives a highly misleading picture of what happened in philosophy from Descartes to Kant. Not one of the early modern philosophers doubted that there is a physical world or denied that natural science gives us knowledge of that world. The real question that ties together the early modern period is what gives scientific knowledge its special character and its special authority for us. Idealism in Kant (and Hegel) is meant to offer not a new account of physical objects but a new account of authority, one that can explain the claims of both scientific knowledge and morality. What makes German idealism distinctive and important is that it seeks to offer an account of authority that depends only on human beings and their own rationality, and not on an independent appeal to God or even to nature.

RATIONALISM AND DIVINE AUTHORITY

A crisis of authority is the occasion for the founding text of modern philosophy, Descartes' *Meditations*. Even before Descartes went into his stove-heated room to meditate, he tells us in a preface that is explicitly addressed to his Jesuit teachers, he came to see that some of the things he was taught and believed in his youth turned out to be false. The goal of the *Meditations* is to offer a new argument for the most basic of Christian religious teachings,

---

[2] Peter Strawson, *The Bounds of Sense: An Essay on Kant's Critique of Pure Reason* (Methuen, 1966), p. 38.

for the existence of God and the immortality of the soul. The implication is clear: the traditional warrant for these teachings is inadequate, and we need a new kind of justification to replace religious authority.

Skeptical doubt in philosophy is not new. Nor is the demand that religious faith be replaced or at least accompanied by rational argumentation. But the way Descartes goes about his skeptical doubt soon makes it clear that his worry about the authority of knowledge is quite different from anything in ancient or medieval philosophy.

In Meditation 1, Descartes offers three different kinds of skeptical argument against the possible validity of the beliefs he now holds. The first is the most traditional: many of his beliefs are based on the senses, and the evidence of our senses often turns out to be deceiving. This is exactly what the ancient skeptics stressed when they argued, for instance, that an object can appear smaller if you see it from a great distance, or warmer if your hand is already cold. But it turns out that these arguments are inadequate for Descartes, because they leave certain basic beliefs about the physical world intact. We may not know the exact nature of the physical objects we sense, but we know enough of them to know that they are there – and to know what they are. "[T]here are many other beliefs about which doubt is quite impossible, even though they are derived from the senses," writes Descartes, "– for example, that I am here, sitting by the fire, wearing a winter dressing-gown, holding this piece of paper in my hands, and so on."[3] The ancient skeptics never would have denied that there was a piece of paper, even if they wondered how we could know its true qualities.

So Descartes then famously imagines that he is dreaming, and thus that the paper is not real. But even this argument is not yet what Descartes is looking for. Even in a dream, he tells us, the images would be made up of certain fundamental qualities, without which we could not have the dreaming thoughts:

. . . it must at least be admitted that certain other even simpler and more universal things are real. These are as it were the real colors from which we form all the images of things, whether true or false, that occur in our thought. To this class of objects seem to belong corporeal nature in general and its extension; the figure of extended things, their quantity or magnitude, and their number, as also the place in, and the time during, which they exist, and other things of the same sort.[4]

---

[3] René Descartes, *Meditations on First Philosophy*, First Meditation, in J. Cottingham, R. Stoothoof, and D. Murdoch (trans.), *The Philosophical Writings of Descartes* (Cambridge University Press, 1988), pp. 12–13.

[4] Descartes, *Meditations on First Philosophy*, First Meditation, in Cottingham et al., p. 14.

Even if Descartes' piece of paper does not exist, his thoughts about it are still composed of certain concepts that make up his understanding of a physical object. The belief in the reality of the paper may be unreliable, but the concepts that comprise the belief in the paper cannot be questioned – unless, Descartes argues, those concepts have been placed into our minds by an evil demon who wishes to distort our understanding. What Descartes really wants us to doubt, then, is not the reliability of our senses, or even the existence of physical objects, but rather the reliability of the concepts we use to think about the world. And this is something that the ancient philosophers never asked us to do.

Like Descartes, Socrates demanded that philosophy appeal only to reason, and thus not to any other sort of authority like tradition or the commands of another person (or even a deity). But Socrates also had a quite specific idea of what reason looked like: it was a definition, an account of a thing's essence. There is some question about whether Socrates was really talking about objects when he discussed moral terms, but Plato and his successors certainly took him to be talking about the nature of things. In that sense, the Platonic view is that to give a rational account of something is to appeal only to its nature or to its essence. Implicit in this view are the assumptions that essences are in some sense out there in the world, waiting to be uncovered, and that our minds are somehow already set up to perceive them. Perceiving them might take a good deal of work, but this work will be a matter of altering ourselves, of ridding ourselves of our prejudices or our reliance on the passions, to prepare us for the encounter with the truth of things. The assumption is that our rational capacity, properly isolated and engaged, already gives us access to that truth.

What this assumption implies is a belief in the reliability of the concepts we use to categorize the world. Since Socrates thought that the operation of rationality consisted in the examination of our concepts, the assumption that our rational capacity is naturally suited to grasp the truth of things amounts to the assumption that our concepts are already adequate to grasp the truth. So though Socrates spends a great deal of time worrying about the proper definitions of words like *friendship* or *justice,* he never seems to question whether these words are the right ones to use when talking about moral reality, or whether we might not do better to use some entirely different set of concepts, words that might divide up the moral world in a very different way. What Descartes' evil demon is meant to suggest is that the concepts we are using now might be entirely misplaced.

Where does this new skeptical thought come from? The standard answer is that Descartes was driven to his search for foundations by a desire to legitimate the discoveries of modern science, to vindicate the newly emerging mathematical physics. But just what is it that makes this form of science so different? Why aren't the calculations and the successful predictions of the mathematical physicists themselves enough? Why do they require some sort of further legitimation?

The deeper answer is that modern mathematical physics does not look like science in the classical and especially in the Aristotelian sense. Again, the traditional Platonic assumption is that a rational (and hence a scientific) account of a thing is an account of its essence. But Plato also assumed that an account of a thing's essence would also explain what the thing's purpose was, what role it played in the world. This is most obvious in his account of moral virtues: in the *Republic*, Socrates demands that we provide an account that tells us not just what justice is but also why it is good for us. But even Thrasymachus' rejected account tells us what justice is for – namely, to advance the interests of unscrupulous rulers. And this teleological assumption persists into Aristotle's account of science: to provide a full explanation of something is to explain what that thing is for. A scientific understanding may look quite different from our ordinary account of a thing, but it is always supposed to make our account of things richer, in the sense of connecting the thing to the rest of life. By contrast, the modern scientific account of the world is in this sense an impoverished account, one that strips away the connection between physical things and any larger purposes. To understand the world as simply a set of particles in mathematically ordered motion, you have to abstract from almost all of the features of objects that give them meaning in the ordinary sense.

Abstraction, in the end, is Descartes' own answer to the question of why a scientific account of the world requires such an apparently impoverished set of concepts. The language of mathematical physics may not be the richest way of understanding an object, but it is, Descartes contends, the most basic way of looking at an object, the one that is presupposed in any way of looking at the world, and even in any dream. This answer is itself presupposed by Descartes' skeptical inquiry, which is in one sense not very skeptical, because it claims to render doubtful all of Descartes' beliefs by doubting certain basic beliefs that are foundational to all the others, a procedure which already assumes that we accept the account of which beliefs are foundational. Extension, Descartes already asserts in Meditation 1, is the most general and basic concept of a physical thing, the one from which it is not possible to abstract away. That much cannot be subject to skeptical doubt.

But in another sense, Descartes' inquiry remains highly skeptical, because he does doubt whether his most basic physical concepts are reliable guides to understanding the world. If an evil demon is responsible for our abstract reasonings, then mathematics and mathematical physics cannot count as authoritative knowledge. In a way, this argument should seem puzzling, because the argument from abstraction already assumes that our basic physical concepts have subjective certainty (we cannot think about the natural world without them), and subjective certainty is supposed to be Descartes' standard of truth. Why, then, does Descartes believe that our abstract, scientific reasonings require a further argument for God's existence, so that the goodness and power of God can prevent the intercession of an evil demon? Readers of Descartes have always been puzzled by this question, because they have worried from the start that Descartes' argument for God's existence relies on a circular appeal to the principle of abstraction that Descartes' God is supposed to be upholding. According to this oldest of objections, Descartes cannot argue from his having the clear and distinct idea of God to the fact of God's existence, because this argument assumes that Descartes can rely on his clear and distinct idea of God, and the reliability of our clear and distinct ideas is exactly what God's existence is meant to guarantee.[5] It is important to see that this objection is not any sort of argument against Descartes' method of abstraction; it is only an argument against appealing to God in order to support that method. Readers who make this objection don't see how the appeal to God is supposed to help. They think that Descartes merely relies on his method of abstraction at every moment, which makes it difficult to understand why he was worried about an evil demon in the first place.

To understand his worry, we need to remember the plainest of facts: what God has, and the demon does not, are goodness and power. God's goodness and power, after all, are what should reassure us that no demon is interfering with the reliability of our abstract reasonings. The difference between our idea of God and our idea of physical substance cannot be a matter of individuating them as concepts; the ideas of God and extension remain exactly what they are throughout the entire course of the *Meditations*. But Descartes clearly thinks that the concept of God is somehow more complete, and that this completeness implies a kind of self-validating quality. And the only qualities that can make something self-validating are goodness and power. Consider the question: why should it be that there is an omnipotent, omnibenevolent God? The answer is already implied in the description of

---

[5] See the argument of the Third Meditation.

the divine nature: so that the good will be done. If you go on to ask why this should be so, you are participating in evil, not raising a deeper rational or skeptical doubt. By contrast, the question of why the universe should consist merely of extended substance governed by mathematical laws is an entirely coherent question, one that raises deep questions about the thinness of the modern scientific view of the world, about its relation to our own ends and values. It is these kinds of questions that the evil demon is meant to suggest. That the idea of extended substance is a conceptually necessary abstraction, that it has subjective certainty for us as we think about the physical world, is not enough to convince us that the world, deep down, is nothing more than a set of particles governed by mathematical laws. Why should we conceive of the world as modern scientists do? This is a question that the scientific outlook, on its own, cannot answer.

Another way of putting this point is to say that scientific concepts, on their own, lack authority, because authority is another name for the combination of goodness and power that Descartes is looking for. An authority is someone who, like God, is empowered to do good; if that person fails to do good, we will say that he or she has failed in his or her role. Because it is a defining feature of modern scientific concepts that they abstract from claims about value, they lack the sort of authority that religion claims to have. It is not yet clear why it is good for us to adopt them. In contrast, Descartes believes that the concept of God has an authoritative power and goodness built into it, and he believes that in a quite literal way: since he argues that only God himself could have placed the idea of an infinitely powerful and good God in our minds, he thinks of our concept of God as itself inheriting some of the power and goodness of God himself. Scientific concepts, in turn, get their authority from God, because an all-powerful and all-good God would not have created us with the abstract concepts that we have to rely on were this reliance not a good thing. The goodness and power of the mathematical abstractions that form the conceptual basis of modern science come from the goodness and power of God, who placed those ideas into our minds.

EMPIRICISM AND NATURAL AUTHORITY

The rationalist account of scientific knowledge is that it consists of deductive, mathematical reasoning from certain abstract concepts, which serve as axiomatic starting points. As a description of what modern physical theories look like, this account is reasonably accurate. But as a description of where those theories come from, of what justifies the supposedly axiomatic starting points, the account doesn't offer very much help. As we have seen, appealing to the conceptual necessity of certain ideas of physical substance can only go so far, because conceptual necessity is not enough to ensure a complete description of the world. The modern scientific view is that everything that happens in the world can be described in mechanistic terms, and that view is not justified by the claim that a particular set of mechanistic concepts is conceptually necessary for us. Why should we believe that even a subjectively necessary concept like extension is enough to explain everything that happens in the world? This question can be put in its narrower and more practically scientific form: can you really do physics with this idea alone? (On this count, Descartes' hope to do without the concept of mass didn't work out all that well.) But the question can also be put in a broader and more philosophical form: how can we be sure that a thin physical concept like extension, even if it turns out to be axiomatic for our physicists' favorite theories, is enough to explain everything that happens? It is at this point that the rationalist account is compelled to appeal to God, to guarantee the authority of the axioms of science.

This kind of view has to walk a very precarious line. On the one hand, rationalism needs to appeal to God to provide science with its authority. On the other hand, rationalism needs to keep God out of scientific practice, to allow modern physics to provide its wholly mechanical explanations. This is why Descartes sees God first giving us our idea of extension, and then our going on to explain the workings of the physical world with this idea alone. But it is not clear that divine authority pervades the idea of extension in the way Descartes really needs. This idea is supposed to carry divine authority because our minds rely on it, and because God has created our minds. We are thus supposed to trust that God has created us well. But God has also created us with unreliable sensory organs, and Descartes is not above arguing also that we ought to trust in God and rely on our senses, if only to a limited extent.[6] What Descartes really needs is not for us to trust in the divine authority of the concept of extension, but for us to be able to see that authority in the concept itself. In Descartes' rationalist successors, this defect is made good: both Leibniz and Spinoza believe that the proper starting point of deductive science is not simply an abstract set of physical ideas but the idea of God itself. But that way of proceeding either smuggles teleological premises back into modern physical science (which was exactly Leibniz's goal) or preserves mechanism by altering the traditional concept of God into something less than an all-good, all-powerful authority

---

[6] See the Sixth Meditation.

(a consequence that Spinoza was willing to accept). In the end, it is not really possible to keep God out of modern science while simultaneously using Him to prop it up.

Ultimately, the other main view in early modern philosophy – the empiricism of Hobbes, Locke, Berkeley, and Hume – offers a far more plausible account of modern scientific authority, precisely because it seeks to do without an appeal to divine authority. It is true that Locke and Berkeley, especially, do understand natural science as revealing the wisdom and goodness of God, but this is merely an effect of scientific practice on us, not something that is needed to practice or justify scientific reasoning itself.

Up to a point, the empiricists are trying to do the same thing as the rationalists: to take an inventory of our concepts, and thereby identify a set of basic, abstract ideas that are foundational for scientific practice. But the empiricist way of legitimating those foundational ideas is very different, and Locke famously starts his *Essay* by attacking Descartes' appeal to innate ideas (ideas that are supposed to come from God and thereby carry divine authority) as dogmatic and unhelpful. The project of empiricism is to legitimate our concepts by tracing them back to certain simple, unmediated, and hence unquestionable sensory experiences. A valid concept is simply a name that we assign to such a sensory experience, or to some complex combination of sensory experiences. If a concept cannot be traced back to some simple set of experiences, then it is a mere word, an artificial human creation that blocks our access to the natural world. (Hobbes, most prominently, identifies those manmade obstacles with the outdated categories of scholastic metaphysics and Aristotelian science.) The task of empiricist philosophy is to strip our language of these artificial distortions, to restore to our language the simplicity of sense-experience.[7] Such a stripped-down language is meant to be suited for scientific practice, since it relies on nothing more than direct observation of the natural world. The authority for scientific concepts is thus provided not by God but by nature, which gives us direct, unmediated access to the physical world.

The advantages of this strategy are considerable. There is no appeal to a divine authority who nonetheless plays no role in scientific practice, and there is a central role for observation and experiment, which has an awkward and uncertain place in the rationalist account, which stresses only abstraction and deductive reasoning. But though it seems right to say that if a concept cannot be connected to observation, it is ill-suited for scientific

---

[7] See John Locke, *An Essay Concerning Human Understanding*, Book III, especially the concluding chapters on the imperfections and the abuse of words, chapters IX–XI.

practice, the reverse does not follow. That a concept derives from our sensory experience does not mean that is does or should play a role in our scientific theories. Descartes was exactly right that the mathematical abstractions of modern physics do not look much like ordinary sensory experience. As Locke was well aware, modern physics regards the direct evidence of many of our senses – colors, sounds, smells – as merely secondary qualities, which are to be explained in terms of primary qualities like figure and extension. At the fundamental level, colors are not "real": they arise from the interaction of colorless particles, from the effect of light on objects and our sensory organs.[8] To an extent, Locke hopes to ground this kind of reduction in a deeper and better sort of observation. He is enthusiastic about telescopes and microscopes, which open up new views of the world, and he muses repeatedly about an especially powerful microscope that would allow us to look directly at the fundamental particles that structure every physical object.[9] But he also seems to realize that even the best possible microscope would not do the job he needs it to do. The problem is not just that the evidence of our senses is potentially shallow and immediate, that it might not survive the explanations of our deepest and best physical theories. The real problem is that the evidence of our senses is always contingent: it always reflects what we have happened to observe rather than the deep and essential structure of nature. Whatever we see in Locke's better microscope will certainly require a deeper explanation to connect it to more macroscopic properties. But whatever we see there will not come with some sort of special warrant that could tell us that we have penetrated to the heart of nature. All we will be able to say is that we saw it – which is, in the end, a fact about *us* and not a fact about the heart of nature.

Locke is most keenly aware of this problem when he distinguishes between the "nominal" and the "real" essence of a substance.[10] One of his favorite examples is "gold," which is, as he tells us, a name for a yellow metal of a certain hardness, which is soluble in *aqua regia,* and so on. That is, the word *gold* stands for a collection of sensations that we have had and group together based on our repeated experiences. But this collection of sensations, this set of properties, does not yet describe the essential nature of the physical substance gold. We know, again, that "yellowness" will not be part of the atomic structure of gold; rather, something about the atomic structure of gold explains why gold appears yellow to us. We will have

[8] Locke, *Essay*, Book II, chapter VIII.
[9] See for instance *Essay*, Book II, chapter XXIII, 11–12.
[10] Locke, *Essay*, Book III, chapter VI.

arrived at the "real essence" of gold when we can identify the essential set of properties that underlie all the other properties of gold. Locke's account here is highly Cartesian: he imagines a process of deductive reasoning that would take us from the real essence of gold to all its other properties, to anything that anyone might include in its nominal essence. But as for the question of how we know that some specified set of properties should count as the real essence of gold, Locke is not sure what to say.[11] Our observations of gold, even under a powerful microscope, remain our observations, and so the properties we identify in those observations remain names that we have assigned to sensations we have happened to have. In other words, anything we would ever call "gold" looks like a nominal essence, a human convention that may or may not correspond to the deeper reality of nature. That one such convention might explain more than another is not enough to get us beyond convention to nature as it is in itself. On the empiricist view, what is supposed to tie our concepts to nature is sensation, but sensation turns out to be contingent on the particular perspective of our experience. Even if they are connected to observation, all our concepts are thus potentially what Hobbes condemned in scholastic metaphysics: merely human inventions that have no essential connection to the true nature of the physical world.

All of the subsequent complications in the British empiricist tradition, all of the skeptical worries raised about Locke's positions by Berkeley and Hume, turn out to be further consequences of this problem about the contingency of our experiential concepts. Berkeley's attack on the distinction between primary and secondary qualities is just a radicalization of Locke's doubts about our ever knowing the real essence of gold: if even the supposed primary qualities included in gold's nominal essence do not necessarily correspond to the real essence of the natural kind, then it is hard to see why we should call those qualities primary at all. That we can explain our sensations of color in terms of sensations involving figure and extension does not make those latter qualities into things that stand apart from all our sensations.[12] This argument, which is repeated over and over again in Berkeley, is supposed to convince us to abandon our idea of "material substance" by driving a wedge between our sensations and the reality they are supposed to represent. The argument functions not because we are tempted to believe that our sensations do not represent reality, but because our sensations do not carry enough authority to overcome their essential

---

[11] See especially *Essay*, Book IV, chapter III.
[12] Berkeley, *A Treatise Concerning the Principles of Human Knowledge*, Part I, 13.

contingency, and thus to provide necessity for any set of scientific concepts. The concepts of "matter" and "primary qualities" look like they are supposed to carry that sort of authority in modern scientific thinking, and that is exactly why Berkeley suggests that a good empiricist should throw them out. Instead Berkeley proposes that we accept that radical contingency of our sensory experience – and then praise God for providing as much order and regularity in our experience as He has. As an attempt to explain the authority of modern science, this last suggestion is about as unhelpful as could be. Leibniz and Spinoza at least associated the concept of God with rational necessity; Berkeley, on the other hand, prefers a more voluntarist conception that makes the order of the physical universe into a free gift to us from God. On this conception of God's role, it is nearly impossible to describe the theories or the discoveries of modern science as any sort of advance in rationality.

Hume is the most radical of the British empiricists not because he understands the contingency of empirical knowledge any more deeply than Locke or Berkeley, but because he simply accepts that contingency for what it is, and is not tempted to wish for any further support, like a special microscope or the continued assistance of a loving God. Hume's most famous argument, his skeptical account of our causal beliefs, is again a kind of application of Locke's worry about nominal essences.[13] We cannot say, Hume tells us, that a cause is necessarily connected with its effect; all we can say is that we have experienced the cause and the effect in repeated succession. The inference to a necessary connection depends on a further assumption that our past experiences will continue to serve as a reliable guide for the future. But this assumption, the general principle of induction, cannot be justified by experience without circularity, and so Hume simply regards it as a brute fact about the natural operation of our minds. That is, he regards causal beliefs as simply contingent generalizations about our particular experiences, just as Locke regarded nominal essences as simply contingent sets of qualities that we associate together and then presume to be natural kinds. In neither case do we reach what Hume called the "secret powers" of objects, the inner workings of nature.

The difference is that Hume is fully comfortable with this conclusion. He is not troubled by the conclusion that causal necessity is simply a subjective quality of our beliefs, not a fundamental feature of the physical world. Even that formulation is really inadequate to describe Hume's thinking, because it is not as if he would have ever denied or even doubted that the physical

---

[13] David Hume, *An Enquiry Concerning Human Understanding*, Sections IV–V.

world is causally ordered. It is not as if we could ever think otherwise. For Hume, the general principle of causality is not something that can be given any sort of justification. In one sense, he sees causal determinism as having a kind of subjective necessity for us, but at the same time, he sees necessity as arising empirically, in the particular beliefs we are conditioned to hold by our particular experiences.[14] In that sense, he refuses any version of Descartes' project of showing that our subjectively necessary concepts have any sort of rational authority. Our tendency to form causal beliefs may be an "innate" feature of our minds, but that doesn't make it rational, and it certainly doesn't make it divinely inspired. All the specific beliefs that our causally oriented minds form are empirical, and they all are contingent and subject to revision. When we believe that a cause leads to an effect, we are always making a kind of assumption of necessity, and we can always be wrong. Hume's empiricism penetrates even into his account of justification: he provides an empirical description of how believers come to see their views as justified, not a justification of the beliefs themselves. On this kind of view, the empiricist project of justification itself drops out: we can no longer validate the commitments of modern physics by saying that they have a special connection to sensory experience. For Hume, all our beliefs arise from experience, and some of those beliefs just turn out, over time, to be more reliable than others. Hume would certainly have agreed with the claims that the modern scientific revolution represented an advance in human thinking, and that modern scientific beliefs are better grounded in experience. But he would not have agreed that these claims give those beliefs any special authority. His picture of the modern scientific revolution is not at all revolutionary. The development of modern physics was just one example of a tendency that characterizes all of human history – the tendency to gradually improve our beliefs by collectively acquiring more and more experience. Modern scientific beliefs have authority for us, but that authority arises naturally in the normal process of belief-formation that is the effect of all our experience.

In that sense, Hume ends the project of early modern philosophy. When he takes an inventory of our concepts, he does not find any that have any special divine, rational, or natural authority. All he sees are contingent sets of concepts in continual revision in the face of experience. The reliability of our concepts thus depends on a kind of general assumption, never questioned by Hume, that as natural creatures, we remain in a basically healthy cognitive relation to the world. So even though our concepts are human

---

[14] Hume, *An Enquiry Concerning Human Understanding*, Sections VII–VIII.

creations that might prove inadequate to grasp the true nature of the world, their artificiality is no reason to subject them to any sort of sweeping critique. Hume's reformist, anti-revolutionary temperament rules that kind of questioning out, despite his deep interest in skeptical arguments. But it is important to see that this is simply a matter of temperament: the naturalist confidence that our beliefs have evolved to grasp the structure of nature is not something that can itself be given any sort of naturalist defense. Naturalism is a property of explanations, not any sort of justification of any particular explanation, and thus no justification of the claim that our current concepts are well suited to comprehend the world. Still, the basic Humean confidence is hard to shake without some compelling skeptical challenge, and as Hume emphasizes in his discussion of skepticism about the existence of physical objects, sweeping skepticism needs more than theoretical possibility to compel us to change our attitude toward the world. The idea that our concepts might be fundamentally inadequate needs some practical force if we are to entertain it seriously. Descartes had asked us to entertain the idea to justify the strangeness of the mathematical abstractions of modern physics, but Hume retains neither the sense that mathematical abstractions are especially strange nor the conclusion that any set of concepts is especially familiar, in that it can be certified, in either Cartesian or Lockean fashion, as truly the mind's own. The Cartesian project of finding some rationally privileged set of concepts needs some practical motivation. By the time of Hume, I have been arguing, the theoretical fortunes of this project were fading, but so was the sense of its theoretical force. Resurrecting it required a different sort of challenge, and this challenge, I now argue, came from developments in moral and political philosophy. This challenge had a different sort of practical force and required a very different kind of solution.

CHAPTER 3

Freedom

I said in Chapter 1 that the German idealists saw the idea of freedom as the central concept of modern philosophy: as symbolic of the problem of rational justification, especially under modern conditions, and, if rightly conceived, as also the solution to this problem. In this chapter, I want to explain how the German idealists were able to use the idea of freedom to reformulate the project of modern philosophy in a new way, in a way that understood the full import of Hume's criticisms of Descartes' and Locke's attempts to establish the authority of our concepts. Hume's insistence on the contingency of all our beliefs suggested to Kant, and then to Hegel, that modern philosophy required a new and different account of authority, one that was centrally connected to the notion of human freedom.

Of course, the idea of freedom was already an important idea in modern moral and political philosophy, especially in the British tradition. By the time of the German idealists, Hobbes and Locke had already insisted on the natural rights of all human beings, and their claims were clearly at work in the Declaration of Independence and the Declaration of the Rights of Man and the Citizen. So what more needed to be done? In what sense does freedom pose a philosophical problem, and in what sense does it require a philosophical solution of the sort offered by Kant or Hegel? To understand this, we need to understand that what Rousseau, Kant, and Hegel mean by freedom is quite different from what Hobbes and Locke had meant. And it is this second sense of freedom that seems to call for philosophical treatment. To understand this point, we are going to have to take an extended detour through the history of the earlier tradition, so that we can appreciate why it was that this second sense of freedom came to seem so important.

PHYSICAL AND MORAL FREEDOM

This earlier history has its special complications, because Hobbes and Locke do not always use the same terminology to talk about freedom. Thus they sometimes seem to disagree, even when their views actually run in the same direction. To simplify things, I am going to concentrate on Hobbes' account, because the distinction between the two types of freedom is already there, even if it is not explicitly described in those terms.

Hobbes begins, in his characteristically naturalist and empiricist way, by defining freedom in strictly physical terms, as a property of objects in motion.[1] A moving object is free, Hobbes tells us, when it is able to persist in its motion without hindrance from external objects. So water is free to flow downstream if it is not blocked by a dam, and a rock is free to roll downhill if it is not blocked by trees or a retaining wall. As for human actions, Hobbes understands them as bodily motions caused by appetites or aversions, by what contemporary philosophers tend to call desires. So human beings are free when their movements to satisfy their desires are not blocked or restricted by external forces, and particularly by the actions of other human beings.

The external restraints that most concern Hobbes are the violent actions of other human beings, which threaten our bodies and our lives. For both Hobbes and Locke, the basic moral and political evil is violence against one's body or, as Locke adds, against one's property – which Locke in fact describes as a kind of physical extension of the body, since for him an object of property literally contains the physical results of one's labor, as reflected in the "improvement" of the object over its original, natural state.[2] It is to eliminate the threat of violence that Hobbes famously urges us to leave the state of nature: to consent to "laws of nature" that allow just as much freedom for other men as one claims for oneself, and then to consent to enter into a commonwealth, to accept a sovereign power that could enforce the laws of nature and thus make it rational for everyone to obey them.[3] Since men living under the laws of nature are free from the violent actions of others, one might call the result of obedience to these laws a state of freedom. That, in fact, is exactly how Locke describes it.[4] But Hobbes does not, because he is also thinking about a second kind of freedom, distinct from physical freedom. Humans who obey the laws of nature may be free of physical threat from other human beings, but they are also living under a series of restraints, namely the obligations imposed by the laws of nature themselves. These laws are "artificial bonds," chains

---

[1] Thomas Hobbes, *Leviathan*, Part II, chapter XXI, 1–2.

[2] Hobbes, *Leviathan*, Part I, chapter XIV, 1–4; John Locke, *Second Treatise of Government*, chapters II and V.

[3] Hobbes, *Leviathan*, Part I, chapters XIV–XV; Part II, chapter XVII.

[4] Locke, *Second Treatise*, chapter II, 4.

imposed by human beings upon themselves in the interest of physical security. They are not physical restraints – though they can be backed up with the physical restraints of the sovereign's punishments – but rather the artificial, normative restraints of moral and legal requirements, created (according to Hobbes) by the contractual agreements of human beings who choose to bind themselves and each other.[5] But they are like physical restraints in that they limit the ability of human beings to do whatever they desire. Locke quotes a brief and not especially convincing argument from Hooker against this point, which attempts to show that all of us really do desire to obey the laws of nature, so that there is no loss of freedom resulting from obedience to moral and political requirements.[6] But for Hobbes, moral and political obligations really do restrain us – not in the physical sense of preventing our bodily movements, but in the internal or "moral" sense of preventing us from simply doing whatever we decide to do.

The difference between the two senses of freedom can be captured by noting that if individuals takes themselves to be obligated to follow a moral or political norm, they are physically free to violate the norm, but they are not rationally free to reject it. Their bodies are free in a sense that their wills are not. To some people, this sounds like a very strange thing to say, because obviously any physically free individual is capable of violating any norm at any time. You can certainly understand and even recognize the goodness of a norm, and yet still act against it; that happens all the time. But the case we are talking about here is not the one in which you violate a norm, but the one in which you conform to it, precisely because you accept it as valid reason for acting. (This case, of course, is what Kant described as acting out of duty.) If you accept a norm and take yourself to be required to obey it, there is a sense in which you do not understand yourself as free to reject it. That is just what your taking yourself to be required to obey it means.

Obviously the next question is how our wills come to be bound by moral or political norms. Hobbes' account of both of these, as we have already noted, is famously contractarian: we have bound our own wills by agreeing with others to obey the laws of nature, and then to obey the commands of the sovereign who will enforce the laws of nature. We enter into these agreements out of self-interest, from a prudential desire to avoid the violence that threatens if the laws of nature are not respected. This argument clearly implies that Hobbes values physical over internal or "moral" freedom, because he is telling us to give up our freedom to reject moral and political norms by binding ourselves to precisely those norms

---

[5] Hobbes, *Leviathan*, Part II, chapter XXI, 5–6.   [6] Locke, *Second Treatise*, chapter II, 5.

which will protect our physical freedom. But as both Hume and Rousseau later came to agree, there is a real question about whether doing this makes any sense, and thus whether a contractarian account of normativity is possible at all.

Remember that the case we are emphasizing is the one in which we understand our wills to be bound by norms. And when we ask why we are so bound, Hobbes' answer is that we have contracted with others to obey the norms. But why are we bound to obey this contract? To appeal to a norm of obedience to contract would be circular: the principle that we should keep our promises is already a normative notion, so we can't appeal to it to explain how we became bound by norms in the first place. That means Hobbes has to fall back on the appeal to self-interest: you should keep our contracts because if you don't, others will feel free to break theirs, and their actions will threaten your physical freedom. There's nothing wrong with that argument in itself, as a directive of prudence, but once again, we can't use it to explain how our wills ever became bound by norms. For if the relevant appeal is to self-interest, then our wills never really become bound at all: even you make a contract, you can and should break the contract if obeying it would threaten your physical security (e.g., if you suspect that others will fail to keep their word, placing those who obey in a position of weakness). And in fact that is exactly what Hobbes – and Locke – say. They both agree that if your government's policies threaten your physical security, you are under no obligation to obey them.[7] But that means that our wills are never really bound to any norms: at every moment, we are free to decide what best protects our physical freedom. (That doesn't mean you should never obey your government, because disobedience carries its own risks, but it does mean that you, and not the government, should be the one to evaluate the risks on either side.) Despite what Hobbes says, on his view, we never in fact surrender our internal or moral freedom. We simply use it to understand how to protect our physical freedom. As accounts of what political institutions are for, of the practical interests that they promote, Hobbes' and Locke's views are perfectly coherent. But as accounts of political obligation, of how it is that individuals come to be bound by political norms, their arguments don't work at all.

THE ARTIFICIALITY OF NORMS

It was exactly this criticism that was raised against Hobbes and Locke by both Hume and Rousseau. The charge of circularity comes straight from

---

[7] Hobbes, *Leviathan*, Part II, chapter XXI, 10–21; Locke, *Second Treatise*, chapter XIX.

Hume's attack on the idea of the social contract, and the same charge is at work in Rousseau's complaint that the British social contract theorists have ruined their arguments by importing back into their accounts of the state of nature notions drawn from the social state.[8] What is imported back is just the idea of normativity – the perceived rightness of some standard of action – such as the principle that we ought to keep our contracts. For Rousseau, and for Hume too, what is interesting and important about normative standards is that they are essentially shared: when we appeal to them, even in our own deliberations, we presume that others will endorse the standards too (a contract is something that everyone knows that everyone is expected to keep).[9] Normativity, then, depends essentially on our social nature, because it is only in a social condition that there are shared standards of value.

This is why Rousseau places so much emphasis on the transition from the state of nature to a social condition, and it explains his notorious and otherwise hopeless claim that the state of nature was essentially a solitary state where nothing bad ever happened.[10] Rousseau does not mean to say, empirically, that there once was a time when human beings never lived with each other and never suffered sickness, injury, or death. When Rousseau says that the state of nature can only be a happy one, he is talking not about the physical impossibility of pain and suffering, but about the conceptual impossibility of a certain sort of pain and suffering outside of human culture. That pain and suffering is the sort caused by comparisons with other human beings, and those comparisons are possible only if humans share standards and frames of reference that all are understood to accept. Rousseau's natural man regards the actions of other human beings as like the effects of the wind and the rain – sources of potential suffering, to be sure, but not something worth protesting about, because for protest to be effective, there has to be an audience that shares the protestor's standards of judgment, and there are no such shared standards among human beings in Rousseau's state of nature, any more than there are between human beings and clouds. Society, though, is shot through with shared standards; for

---

[8] Hume, "Of the Original Contract"; Jean-Jacques Rousseau, *Discourse on the Origin of Inequality*, Introduction.

[9] At the start of Part II of the *Discourse on the Origin of Inequality*, Rousseau writes: "The first person who, having enclosed a plot of land, took it into his head to say *this is mine* and found people simple enough to believe him, was the true founder of civil society" (*The Basic Political Writings*, trans. D. Cress [Hackett, 1987]). It is the belief of others that is crucial, the shared social judgment that the claim to possession has normative validity.

[10] Rousseau, *Discourse on the Origin of Inequality*, Part I.

Rousseau, to have the standards of other people in your mind is just what it means to be a social being. This was the same point that fascinated Hume about moral judgment: when something bad is done to another person, you feel bad too, and so does every other well-socialized person. The injury was not done to you, and so you shouldn't feel any pain; but in a real sense, you do. Your standards of conduct are offended, and so you and the injured party and everyone else react by feeling the same way.[11]

For both Hume and Rousseau, normative standards are socially created: just as Freud would come to say, your conscience is like the voice of all the other people in society, talking in your own head. This is what makes Hume and Rousseau decisively modern, separating them sharply from their predecessors in the history of moral and political philosophy. A great many philosophers, from Plato to Aquinas to the British "moral sense" theorists from whom Hume himself emerged, had understood the capacity for moral judgment as a kind of higher or separate faculty, distinct from the passions or physical appetites. But for all of these earlier thinkers, this higher faculty was still an essentially natural capacity. Even if it was given to us by God, the higher moral faculty was always described as a use, even if an enhanced use, of our capacity for rationality or fellow-feeling, and the full use of the capacity was understood to represent the highest form of human flourishing, the natural purpose of human beings. Hume and Rousseau don't buy any of that. For them, moral standards are social standards, and social standards are only effective if they are collectively internalized, which is just what happens when people grow up in a society. Collective standards don't serve your basic natural purpose; they serve society's purposes, and those purposes are artificial. They have to be created in you; or more precisely, you have to be created or educated to serve them. Hume does think that all the virtues are built on a natural capacity: the faculty of sympathy, the natural tendency that is at work when we wince at the sight of another person's injury. And he thinks that there are natural as opposed to artificial virtues; there are traits of character that we praise as producing effects that we regard as useful to ourselves – or more precisely, as effects that would be useful to ourselves were we in the position to benefit from them. But as that last qualification suggests, what transforms the useful effects into a natural virtue is the response of uninvolved spectators; it is the social praise of the useful effects that is the distinctive feature of moral judgment. Even in the case of the natural virtues, society is already at work ratifying individual judgments of utility, and in that sense, every virtue has an artificial

---

[11] Hume, *An Enquiry Concerning the Principles of Morals*, Section V.

element: our moral praise of that virtue is a social device to promote the collective welfare. Hume's artificial virtues are simply those in which collective welfare is given explicit priority over our sympathetic feelings. Those feelings, Hume thinks, are too weak to serve as any sort of effective moral standard; with sympathy alone, we would have to see harm to condemn it. So sympathy needs to be tutored, to be buttressed with general rules and principles that summarize society's prescriptions for avoiding harm. For Hume, a mature moral agent follows those artificial rules and principles, not just his or her sympathetic feelings, and even overrides those feelings when society's more general rules point the other way.

Up to a point, Rousseau says exactly the same thing. He agrees that even in the state of nature, there is a kind of innate tendency to virtue, which he calls pity, the sympathetic capacity to be affected by the suffering of another human being. And he agrees with Hume that this capacity is too weak to serve as a socially effective standard of action, so culture is constantly overriding it with its own standards. But the way Rousseau puts this point reveals his vast distance from Hume. For Rousseau, a typical example of the way culture supplants pity is the way wealthy people are able to insulate themselves from observing the lives of the poor, so they are not troubled by physical suffering as they concentrate on the pursuit of social status. In this kind of case, of course, culture's role is to suppress virtue, not to enhance it. Behind this example stands the thought that drives all of Rousseau's writings, a thought that, despite all of his skeptical doubts, seems not to have troubled Hume at all: if normative standards are socially imposed standards, if that voice in your head is not your own, natural voice but society's artificially implanted voice, then somebody else is telling you what to do, and there is no reason to believe that that somebody is looking out for your own or even anyone's good. If you listen to that voice, thinks Rousseau, you are really just trying to please other people, and there is nothing more servile and degrading than living your life that way. Since the defining feature of social life is the imposition of normative standards, Rousseau understands living with other people as an endless series of opportunities for degradation, on all sides. Social approval doesn't get you anything for yourself, but neither does it get anything for the people you are trying to impress. The weak have to suck up to the powerful, because they need the approval of the powerful to survive, but at the same time, the powerful have to suck up to the weak, because the sucking up of the weak is what their power consists of. It is sometimes said that Rousseau thinks society is corrupt, but corruption tends to have a point: you pretend to believe in a normative standard, even as you get to manipulate and selectively ignore it for your own gain. For Rousseau, everyone has to follow normative standards, and nobody gains.

On this point, Hume and Rousseau are so far apart that argument between them is hardly even possible. Hume does point out, rather sweetly, that sociability tends to be a nice thing. You do things that please another person, they are pleased with you, and you enjoy their being pleased with you and the pleasant things they tend to do for you in return. Everyone feels good, and what is the harm in that? But a view like Rousseau's can grant that sociability can have its pleasures, just as a view like Hume's can admit that having to flatter the rich and powerful can feel like an exercise in humiliation. Both of these experiences are natural consequences of being influenced by the opinions and approval of others. It's not clear how appealing to either experience could somehow be decisive, unless one had a further argument that could show that one of them was somehow fundamental, while the other was derivative. And it's not clear that either Hume or Rousseau has an argument of this kind, beyond their tendencies to lean in sharply opposing directions. When it comes to the general function of normative standards, Hume's basic attitude is a kind of genial conservatism, a sense that received moral and political principles reflect the wisdom of historical experience; they are devices that have been shown to provide mutual benefit over the long term. (As we saw in Chapter 2, this is exactly the sort of attitude that Hume holds toward our theoretical or scientific beliefs.) In this sense, Hume is the model for today's evolutionary moral theorists, who regard altruistic tendencies as beneficial to the survival of the species. Like those contemporary theorists, Hume wants to reconstruct Hobbes' arguments for the laws of nature so that they don't require any explicit contractual commitment; he retains the idea that norms of honesty and fair dealing are mutually advantageous, but he sees our commitment to those norms as a historically evolved outcome rather than the result of a volitional act.

But evolutionary moral theory is notorious for trying to do justification in reverse. Rather than taking an accepted standard of justification – say, the idea of mutual benefit – and then arguing that a specific norm is the one that follows from that idea, evolutionary moral theory tends to take an existing norm and then construct a story about why that norm could be mutually beneficial. The rightness of existing norms is taken for granted, which is why evolutionary moral theory seems convincing enough for uncontroversial moral norms, like truth-telling, but totally unhelpful for areas of morality that are contested or rapidly changing, like sexual morality, an area in which evolutionary moral theorists have a special talent for embarrassing themselves. Hume is a model here too; he argued that a sexual double standard, under which male promiscuity was tolerated but female promiscuity was punished severely, made a lot of sense.[12] That's the problem with genial conservatism: it assumes that things are basically all right, which is fine until there you are faced with change or controversy, and life puts pressure on you to make a hard decision. Then it's in no way helpful to be told just that things will work out fine in the end. And so the things that Hume says about the general function of normative standards aren't enough to put aside the suspicions of someone like Rousseau, who sees normative standards as alternately like Thrasymachus did, as inventions of the powerful to advance their own power, or like some sort of natural calamity that befell the human race, causing everyone to be distracted from the good life by the voices of other people clamoring in our heads. (Religious conservatives were right to be scandalized by Rousseau: he thought that there was an original sin, but that it wasn't anyone's fault.)

This isn't to say Rousseau has any more general argument for his view than Hume does. He doesn't, but the fact that no general argument is available on either side means that when we are faced with any particular normative standard, there is a real question about whether we should obey it. To see Rousseau as pressing this question is to see the way in which the claims of Hume and Rousseau manage to drive a wedge between the two parts of Hobbes' position. On the one hand, Hobbes wants to tell a particular story about the purpose of norms, namely that they serve to protect physical security and physical freedom. On the other hand, he wants to leave each individual free to assess the value of norms. The link between the two views is supposed to be the contractarian account of normativity: because we understand Hobbes' story about the point of norms, we freely choose to be bound by them. Together, Hume and Rousseau argue that the link won't hold: we can't choose to be bound by norms because they are already socially imposed on us. So it looks like we have to choose between one side or the other of Hobbes' view. Hume opts for the first: he sketches a utilitarian account of the social evolution of norms, and then suggests that the fact that we really didn't choose to be bound by them just doesn't matter all that much. Rousseau, by contrast, opts for the second: no matter what economic or technological improvements social norms make possible, they can't be justified unless it could be shown that we would freely choose them. For his own part, Rousseau despairs of ever showing that, although

[12] Hume, *A Treatise of Human Nature*, Book III, Part II, chapter 12.

he does provide a familiar picture of what such justification would look like: Hobbes' original idea of the social contract, now redescribed not as a historical act or a prudential bargain, but as a moral condition. For Rousseau, and later for Kant, Habermas, and Rawls, the social contract is an idealized agreement in which all individuals freely agree to be bound by norms and, by doing so, do not surrender but preserve their freedom. On this sort of view, the basic moral value is not the physical benefits that justified norms might provide, but the freedom of all individuals to choose norms for themselves.

THE VALUE OF AUTONOMY

It is at this point that the philosophical problem of freedom – the problem of Kant and of later German idealism – starts to make sense. For if there is a basic moral value in our choosing norms for ourselves, then there is a basic question about whether there is any moral value at all, because there is a question about whether the idea of our choosing norms for ourselves makes any sense. As Hume and Rousseau have already suggested, it looks like society chooses norms for us. If we understand Kant as worrying about the consequences of this point, then his emphasis on the problem of freedom starts to look quite different from the way that emphasis is frequently understood in Anglo-American philosophy. It is often said that Kant's fundamental concern is to reconcile human freedom with physical determination. He is concerned with that problem, but it is important to see that the problem becomes crucial for him only because he is also thinking about Rousseau's problem about social norms. The problem of freedom and determinism is a very old one, extending back at least to medieval thought, and there it was traditionally resolved by saying that even though God knows exactly what we are going to do and is in some sense the cause of all that happens, we are still to blame for our evil actions, because we acted against a standard that we knew to be the correct one. On this kind of view, the question of whether we or God or our physical nature really caused the action is beside the point, because we and God all knew and still know that our action was bad and thus deserving of punishment. The norms we carry around in our heads are taken to point to our ultimate good, and so the question of whether we are really free as we obey them can be safely shunted aside. It is only when Rousseau asks whether we really should be responsive to our normative nature that Kant takes it as his problem to show that despite the facts of physical and social determination, we really are free, and free even as we are bound by norms.

Rousseau's emphasis on the artificiality of social norms is what allows Kant to turn Hume's insistence on the contingency of our theoretical and moral beliefs into a philosophical crisis. To provide authority for the thin but supposedly foundational concepts of modern physics, Descartes and Locke turned inward, searching the mind for some basic, rationally privileged set of concepts that would, with the authority of God or of nature, guide all our knowledge of the world. After Hume, that project no longer seemed viable. No external warrant, divine or natural, could provide our ideas with rational necessity, because on Hume's account, necessity is something that arises empirically – and thus contingently – within our ideas themselves. To believe in causal necessity is to believe, based on repeated experience, that a given effect will follow a given cause. To believe in moral necessity is to believe, based on the common judgments of other human beings, that a given action is worthy of praise or condemnation, because it is likely to produce benefit or harm. In neither case is there a guarantee that the necessary connection is real. Subsequent experience can always sever the link that we presume to hold. Necessity is subjective, something that happens in us; it is not any sort of objective property of the physical or metaphysical world. So what underwrites our claims to physical or moral necessity? Hume's answer is his genial conservatism, his basic confidence that our common human experience and our common physical and social natures will always produce beliefs that are, despite occasional exceptions, basically reliable guides to the physical and moral universes. Rousseau's contribution is to challenge Hume's confidence in moral and political terms, in the way a global theoretical skepticism never could. That our theoretical beliefs require a kind of global warrant, a general account of their authority, is a difficult thought to entertain, because entertaining it requires our entertaining sweeping skeptical scenarios in which physical objects turn out to be nothing more than illusions. As I argued in the previous chapter, Descartes was able to entertain those scenarios only by pressing very hard on the differences between the mathematical abstractions of modern physics and the ordinary evidence of our senses. In the subsequent history of early modern philosophy, this distinction was itself subject to severe criticism, and none of Descartes' successors could take his kind of skeptical arguments as seriously as he did (an important reason that it is wrong to understand Cartesian skepticism about the external world to be the chief problem of modern philosophy). But Rousseau's skepticism about social norms is different, because it is specifically practical, and especially because the kind of challenge it raises is one that arises quite naturally in the practical realm. The claim that a moral or political norm is simply a construct of society, and one that does not necessarily serve our own best interests, is a basic move in any sort of moral and political criticism. We can always raise the question of whether a particular moral or political standard is really good, and thus whether we have any reason to obey it.

It might not seem that Rousseau's critique is at all new, because it looks like he is just saying to someone like Hume what Thrasymachus said to Socrates: morality is just something that the powerful put into our heads for their own benefit, so we don't have a good reason to listen to what our heads might be telling us. But in his response to Thrasymachus, Plato too assumes that the social voice in our heads can and should be put to the side: the real question is just whether the life that Thrasymachus praises, the life of the tyrant, is better than a life like Socrates'. The real question, then, is just what it is rational to do, and then the Platonic rationalist will go on to argue that moral behavior is just one part of being rational. And being rational, from Socrates on, has traditionally meant having an account of the nature or essence of things. Since neither Plato nor Thrasymachus assumes that the socially constructed or artificial part of morality is part of its essence, the question of whether we should listen to what society is telling us to do is beside the point. The only question is how things really are. But we have seen that Rousseau, like Hume, does think that the constructed or artificial part of morality is part of its essence – which really means that, in the traditional sense, morality doesn't have an essence at all. Norms are not part of the nature of things. And so any traditionally rationalist account, a view like Plato's or Leibniz's, is going to miss the point of Rousseau's challenge. When Plato and Leibniz think about norms, they don't worry about other people telling us what to do, because they don't think that a rational being would be concerned with what anyone else tells them, except insofar as it bears on the question of what is rational. The issue of freedom drops away, and we are left with a problem about the rationality of moral norms. For Plato, the story Thrasymachus tells about how society duped us into acting morally is really just a device to get at the real issue, which is whether moral action is good or bad for us. But for Rousseau, the duping is the whole problem: he doesn't think we can get at the goodness or badness of what society has taught us, other than to say that things were good before society taught us, and bad now that it has. The challenge is not to show that morality is good for us, but to show that we can respond to moral or social demands without compromising our capacity for independent judgment. So it won't work to argue, as Plato and Leibniz do, that freedom is just the capacity for rational judgment, and morality just one of the things that can be judged to be rational. The only way to answer Rousseau's challenge is to argue that morality and rationality are in some sense forms of freedom. Without that, the claim that morality is rational would make no sense, because if the modern, socially constructed account of morality is right, this claim would amount to saying that we should independently judge that we should surrender our independent judgment. And this is exactly the part of Hobbes' view that Rousseau tells us makes no sense.

On the kind of contractarianism that Rousseau favors, moral and political norms are the expression of free and independent agents, not those agents' subjection to an alien authority. This is also what is expressed by Kant's conception of autonomy: a moral agent turns out to be a free agent, legislating principles for a community of similarly free agents. Necessity, on this kind of view, arises from the voluntary commitments of free individuals. It is important to understand, in one sense, how deeply Humean this view is. Kant actually agrees with the claim that necessity is something that arises subjectively; it is a fact about us, not something that can be found in the world. The essential contingency of our beliefs, the critical weapon that Hume wielded against Descartes and Locke, is overcome not by an external appeal to God or to nature, but by an internal appeal to our nature as subjects. And that nature as subject consists in our identity as free agents, capable of independent judgment. The name for this kind of position is idealism. Its main project is not to show that physical objects are somehow created by our minds, but rather to show that the authority for both our theoretical and our practical beliefs is provided by our nature as free and rational beings.

CHAPTER 4

Idealism

In the previous chapter, I argued that Rousseau's challenge to Hobbes' contractarian account of normativity created a second, specifically philosophical problem of freedom. Freedom was a crucial category in Hobbes' and Locke's accounts of morality and politics, but their primary understanding of freedom was a straightforwardly physical and thus philosophically unproblematic notion of freedom: freedom from the physical restraints of external forces, and particularly of the physical violence of other human beings. This understanding of freedom poses no theoretical difficulties, and so the challenges that Hobbes and Locke faced were mainly practical or political: they had to convince people that moral norms and political institutions existed just to protect people from physical harm, and not to serve any "higher" ethical or religious ends. That project was quite radical, in its way, but carrying it out did not require any special philosophical work.

Rousseau's problem, by contrast, requires a very different sort of solution. Unlike Hobbes or Locke, he was not trying to argue for a new account of the end or goal of moral and political norms. Instead he was arguing that an essential feature of those norms – their socially imposed nature – suggested that they were all invalid, no matter what account anyone gave of their end or goal. For no matter what beneficial social purposes moral and political norms might be taken to serve, those purposes would still be social purposes, and thus they would be imposed on each of us as individuals. The task therefore is to show that each of us can somehow freely accept what is, as an empirical matter, simply imposed on us by socialization. This requires more than making moral and political norms sound especially attractive: it requires a theoretical argument that our individual freedom of choice is somehow compatible with the obvious facts of physical and social determination. The tradition that defined itself by trying to provide such an argument began with Kant, and is now known as German idealism.

45

FREEDOM AND RATIONALITY

The crucial feature of Kant's position – and a defining feature of all forms of German idealism, Hegel's included – is the view that freedom and rationality are deeply and essentially connected. Freedom may seem threatened by the fact of physical determination, but it is less clear that physical causality undermines our capacity for rationality – especially if one assumes, as Kant did, that the scientific study of physical causality is itself an important expression of our capacity for rationality. (Kant presumed that his empiricist or naturalist opponents agreed with this as well; the rise of strongly anti-realist or anti-rationalist accounts of science was a later development.) For Kant, the causes of our thoughts or our actions are one thing, and the justifications for them are another; the former have a physical existence, but the latter exist in a space of reasons. And in that space of reasons, what matters is the rightness of a standard of belief or of action, not the causal history of that standard. And it is a rational being's judgment of rightness – not anything about his or her physical condition – that constitutes his or her freedom. This is what allows Kant to say that people who act out of duty are really free: they freely judge that a moral standard is the correct one, and then bind themselves to the results of their rational deliberations. Obligation might look like constraint, but it is really just the effect of our own rational judgments.

None of this, however, does anything to distinguish Kant from the familiar rationalist accounts of morality that run from Plato through Aquinas to Leibniz. And in one sense, Kant does want to appropriate their rationalism, because none of these thinkers were troubled by the problem of determinism, and Kant wants to get around that problem in exactly the way that they did. Just as Leibniz did not object that God was bound to create the best of all possible worlds, so we should not object when moral agents are bound to follow norms that are rationally justified. But many readers of Leibniz were troubled that his God was not free, and therein lies the crucial point: a view like Leibniz's is saying that everything that is worth caring about in the idea of freedom is reducible to the idea of rationality. That's a fully coherent view, but it does deny that freedom is itself any kind of independent value; and as we saw at the end of the last chapter, without that further claim, we don't have any effective response to a specifically modern critique like Rousseau's.

The deep, original, and important part of Kant's view, then, is not that he assimilates freedom and morality to rationality, but rather that he proposes a radically new conception of rationality, one that includes freedom (and, he argues, morality) as part of its essential nature. Even that formulation is inadequate to the radical novelty of Kant's view, because as we have already noted, on the traditional view, to be rational is to come to understand a thing's essential nature. And the essence of a thing is standardly taken to reside in the object itself. In that sense, the traditional view is that being rational has nothing to do with being free, beyond sloughing off the chains of false opinions and theories; to be rational is to let the true nature of the object guide one's thought. On this kind of view, it makes no sense to describe rationality, or anything else, as essentially free, because both reason and essential natures have to do with the fixed and unchanging properties of objects. What Kant is saying, against the whole weight of the Platonic heritage of Western philosophy, is that being rational ultimately is not about understanding the independent nature of the objects of the world. The study of such objects, natural science (and no longer metaphysics), may be one expression of rationality, but what rationality is in itself is something very different.

To understand Kant's positive view, it helps to start with a rather general and unremarkable observation: if we did have a rational account of something, then all rational persons would agree that this account was the right one. On a traditional view, this agreement is a derivative result: it is the rationality of the account, grounded in the true nature of the thing, that compels the agreement of all rational persons. Kant wants to reverse this traditional priority; he wants to start not with the nature of the object, but with the goal of agreement. Rationality, he believes, is a matter of seeking an account that all persons would freely accept. On this view, rationality refers primarily to persons and to their commitment to a value, the value of agreement, rather than to accounts and the things they are meant to describe.[1] (This is the reason that Kant says that practical or moral reasoning is the primary or full expression of human reason, while theoretical or scientific is a secondary or incomplete use.) Now this claim about the value of agreement may not seem to amount to very much; even if agreement is a good thing to have, we would like to know something about what the basis of that agreement could be. And here Kant does not seem to have advanced at all beyond Rousseau's formula of the social contract: the agreement is just one that everyone freely makes. But Kant does think he can go further,

---

[1] See especially Kant's little but justly famous essay, "What Is Enlightenment?," in which rationality is understood in terms of the audience for and not the content of its claims, and this striking passage from the *Critique of Pure Reason* (A738/B766): "For reason has no dictatorial authority; its verdict is always simply the agreement of free citizens, of whom each one must be permitted to express, without let or hindrance, his objections or even his veto."

because he thinks a person committed to realizing this free agreement is thereby committed to a kind of formal principle: if you put forward a claim as rational, it must be one that everyone else could also freely accept. And this formal claim, Kant thinks, has substantive consequences, in both the theoretical and practical realms. In theoretical reasoning, or reasoning about the nature of things, it means that a claim about an object must be grounded in properties that could be perceived by any observer; in other words, claims about objects must only be empirical claims. In practical reasoning, or reasoning about the goodness of actions, the formal claim means that if you claim that an action is good to do, that action must also be one that all other persons could see as good; that is, it must be possible for all other agents to do that action as well. These claims, of course, are drastic oversimplifications of the arguments that Kant develops in the *Critique of Pure Reason*, the *Groundwork of the Metaphysics of Morals*, and the *Critique of Practical Reason*. Kant's account of empirical or scientific reasoning, and his account of moral reasoning, are complex enough to inspire lifetimes of study. But for now our point can only be that the richness and novelty of these Kantian accounts, the reason we can speak of "Kantian accounts" of science and of morality, is that Kant holds an especially distinctive view about the nature of rationality: that it derives not from the true nature of things, but from our own commitment to reach agreement among ourselves.

A traditional name for this position is "idealism." Kant does not believe, like Berkeley, that objects are somehow ideas in our own minds, but he does believe, in a sense, that the essences of those objects are in our minds, because the norms that govern what it would mean to give a rational account of an object's (or an action's) essential nature come from us rather than from the objects themselves. The world does not impose the norms of science and morality on us; we impose those norms on the world, starting from our own commitment to the idea of free and universal agreement. And this is meant to be Kant's answer to the problem that Rousseau, thinking about Hobbes, had raised: how is it possible that we can freely agree to be bound by norms, if being bound by norms means that we surrender our own judgment to that of society's? In response, Kant is saying that the right norms are just those that derive from the possibility of free agreement. In constraining our judgments to those norms, he is arguing, we are not surrendering to the judgments of others, but expressing our own nature as free and rational beings, who can make rational judgments for ourselves.

This way of understanding Kant places particular emphasis on his moral and political views, and as Onora O'Neill, who has done much to develop it, has stressed, the more general account of rationality is most evident in what might seem to be marginal Kantian texts, such as the little essays "What Is Enlightenment?" and "What Is Orientation in Thinking?," and in the political metaphors that Kant uses at the start and the end of the *Critique of Pure Reason*.[2] (A favorite text of O'Neill's is the much shorter and seldom discussed Doctrine of Method that constitutes the second and final part of the first *Critique*.) On what seem to be more standard readings of Kant, the norms of science and morality are grounded not in the value of public agreement, but rather in arguments about what must be presumed if we are to make claims to empirical knowledge and claims of moral obligation. And on many such readings, reason is not concerned essentially with achieving public agreement, but only with orienting and ordering our own thoughts into a coherent whole. Though the interpretation of Kant's views is obviously not our main concern in this book, I do want to explain why those more standard understandings of Kant, though not wrong in themselves, are nonetheless insufficient, because that explanation will help us understand what the later German idealists valued in Kant's position, and why they came to regard it as insufficient as well.

Especially on many analytic accounts of Kant's theoretical philosophy, the most important (and most effective) arguments of the *Critique of Pure Reason* are understood to be those found in the Transcendental Aesthetic and the Analogies of Experience, in which Kant argues that the claims that the world is spatio-temporal and causally ordered are not propositions that could be verified in experience; rather they are thoughts that must already be presupposed if we are to make any coherent judgments about experience. The important thing to notice about these arguments is that their claims are hypothetical: if they succeed, they ground certain norms of empirical or scientific knowledge, but only on the assumption that our experience does yield such knowledge. This is an assumption that most Anglo-American philosophers, who are already committed to scientific naturalism, are willing to grant from the start. In the Aesthetic and the Analogies, Kant grants it too, but he also worries (in the Transcendental Deduction) about showing how such knowledge is possible, and (in the Dialectic) about showing

---

[2] Onora O'Neill, *Constructions of Reason* (Cambridge University Press, 1989), especially the first two essays, "Reason and Politics in the Kantian Enterprise" and "The Public Use of Reason"; "Vindicating Reason," in Paul Guyer (ed.), *The Cambridge Companion to Kant* (Cambridge University Press, 1992), pp. 280–308; "Constructivism in Rawls and Kant," in Samuel Freeman (ed.), *The Cambridge Companion to Rawls* (Cambridge University Press, 2002), pp. 347–367; and "Autonomy, Plurality and Public Reason," in Natalie Brender and Larry Krasnoff, *New Essays on the History of Autonomy* (Cambridge University Press, 2004), pp. 181–194.

that this knowledge should count as rational, given that it falls short of the traditional philosophical aspiration to full rational explanation. These are not the kind of worries that particularly trouble naturalist readers of Kant. If those readers are impressed with Kant's arguments for the presuppositions of empirical knowledge, they tend to regard those presuppositions as somehow part of the physical architecture of the human brain, in a way that could (eventually) be identified by neurology and the other cognitive sciences, and explained in terms of the evolutionary advantages that this particular cognitive architecture has provided. These accounts would, on the naturalistic view, address both of Kant's worries (which are not really so worrisome, since the naturalist tends also to assume that these scientific accounts will be available in the not-so-distant future). The neuropsychological description would amount to showing how our empirical knowledge is possible, and the evolutionary story would amount to a naturalistic justification of that knowledge.

Neither of these accounts, however, would satisfy Kant, who is trying to understand and account for the normative character of empirical knowledge, and who assumes from the start that experience (and thus any sort of naturalistic account) could not yield the necessity and universality that are the distinctive features of rational norms. So Kant believes he needs an argument like that of the Transcendental Deduction (which most Anglo-American interpreters judge to be a failure, and not an especially troubling failure), in which he argues that our judgments of experience are made possible by an original act of apperception, by the subject's unification of experience into a coherent whole. The nature of this original act of apperception, of course, remains highly obscure (even to Kant), but even if some sort of sense can be made of it, there is still Kant's second problem of showing that the empirical judgments that apperception makes possible should count as rational. In the Dialectic, Kant's answer to that second problem is to argue that unless we grant *both* that all our knowledge is empirical *and* that there can be a fully rational account that is not empirical (i.e., unless we distinguish between appearances and things in themselves), we will be trapped in a series of endless and irresolvable metaphysical disputes. The critical solution is thus to ground the normativity of empirical knowledge in a non-empirical account that is itself not knowledge (because, on this view, all knowledge is empirical). But if normativity cannot be known, then where can we find it? Kant's answer is: in the free activity of the rational agent. We do not know that empirical knowledge is normative; instead, we enact that normativity – in a way that is parallel to the original act of apperception, which is an act, not a fact, that makes judgments of fact possible – by adopting regulative rules for the expansion of our knowledge

through experience. The shift of focus from knowledge to action is crucial here, and it is the same shift that is apparent in Kant's claims that
moral judgments have a kind of final rational justification that scientific
claims never do. Practical and not theoretical reason is the full expression
of human rationality. Normativity is to be found in the nature of rational
action, including the nature of the activity of theoretical reasoning, which
is given a regulative and not a constitutive justification.

If the more familiar readings of Kant were right, then all Kant would
need to do is identify the basic norms of empirical knowledge (and, in the
practical realm, the basic norms of morality, which are often conceived of
in analytic ethics simply as a series of existing intuitions). But as all the
later German idealists knew very well, Kant's deeper project was also to
account for the normativity of theoretical and practical norms, to provide
them with a full rational justification. His special way of doing that was
to link normativity and rationality to the nature of free action, and it thus
becomes essential to show that there really are norms of free action. The
claim that the categorical imperative is the principle that a free and rational
agent would adopt thus becomes, as O'Neill rightly emphasizes, the central
claim of all of Kant's thought, the principle of all autonomous reasoning.
Both moral and scientific reasoning count as reasoning, and get their claims
to normativity, through their connection to the idea of standards that could
be freely adopted by all agents.

The sequence of the claims is crucial here. If the argument is to work, it
has to start from a conception of ourselves as free (as agents capable of independent judgment), then move to a more robust conception of ourselves
as legislators (as proposing claims that could be accepted by all others), and
finally to a substantive set of norms (for Kant, those of scientific and moral
reasoning). Both of these moves are highly controversial. But it is the first
stage of argument that is the more problematic since the second stage is
more straightforwardly a matter of content. The question at the second
stage of argument is whether some sort of Kantian legislative test, some
sort of publicity or universalization requirement, has enough normative
force to lead to some recognizable picture of scientific or moral reasoning.
Even if such a requirement can only go a limited distance, though, it does
seem clear that it is a real normative requirement. Hegel does sometimes
denounce Kant's universalization argument against promise-breaking as
empty; he suggests that there would be nothing inconsistent about a world
in which no one ever intended to keep a promise.[3] But it also seems clear
that Hegel has misinterpreted Kant in these passages: Kant's claim is not

---

[3] Hegel, *Philosophy of Right*, 135R; *Encyclopedia Logic* 54.

that there is anything logically incoherent about a world without mean-ingful promises, but rather that there is something practically incoherent about understanding a promise-breaker's maxim as a legislative claim. If all of us followed the rule of breaking promises whenever it suited us, no one could get anyone else to rely on a (false) promise, which is exactly what the promise-breaker hoped to do. There is something incoherent about a person who makes a promise, and thereby seems to commit himself or herself to the public or legislative claim that promise-keeping is a good thing, and who then goes on to break that promise, thereby contradicting the legislative claim. Inconsistent behavior is a recognizable moral wrong, although only if we take it as a premise that one's actions stake out, at least in cases where others are clearly affected, a kind of normative com-mitment to the goodness of those actions. Despite his criticisms of Kant's account of promise-breaking, Hegel does accept that claim. He does think that our actions imply normative stances for which we are responsible: if I act in ways that suggest to others a normative standard that I then go on to violate, there is something morally wrong with me. So there is clearly some normative force to a universalization or publicity requirement, once we recognize the idea of seeing a person's own commitments as potentially legislative for all others as itself a normative idea.

That it really is a normative idea, however, is certainly not a matter of logical consistency. It is true that if I take an action to be good, I do logically imply the claim that it is good for anyone (in a relevantly similar position) to do. But there is nothing inconsistent about my doing something and also hoping, or even working to ensure, that others do not get to do what I am doing – even as I agree that it would in fact be good for them to do. If we think this is wrong, it is only because we already accept the normative claim that our own standards of conduct are already publicly legislative, as implying standards not just for ourselves but also for all others. But there is still a question about the source of that claim, and so it is better (as Allen Wood has argued) to see Hegel's worry about Kantian emptiness to be a worry about the source of the legislative ideal as a normative claim.[4] The more problematic step in Kant's argument is thus the first: the move from a conception of ourselves as free to the normative conception of ourselves as public legislators. That move, Hegel is justified in saying, is not a matter of logical consistency. Nor can it rely, given Kant's critique of the Platonic conception of rationality, on any appeal to the nature of anything outside of ourselves. Rather, Kant has to argue that the normative

4 Allen Wood, *Hegel's Ethical Thought* (Cambridge University Press, 1990), pp. 154–173.

ideal of ourselves as public legislators (to use the language that Christine Korsgaard has proposed) is already part of our identities as free agents who can make independent judgments for ourselves.[5]

SELF-GROUNDING

The problem with Kant's argument is this: if we take ourselves to be free agents, capable of making judgments for ourselves, why must we judge that the ideal of public legislation is the right one? In my earlier sketch of Kant's account of rationality, I took as a premise the goal of standards that all would freely agree to or, more precisely, the idea of agents practically committed to such a goal. But what is the source of this commitment? Why just assume this as a premise? For Kant's answer to Rousseau's challenge to work, the commitment has to come from the nature of our free agency itself. The scientific and moral norms that we go on to derive must have their ultimate justification in our own freedom. This is the problem that obsessed the later German idealists: how to make our normative commitments "self-grounded." In this context, the search for self-grounding means more than just the traditional search for a standard of justification that would not need support from any further standard, a standard that could ground itself. The later German idealists think they already know what that self-justifying standard is: it is the self, which is free to judge. For them, a self-grounded norm is one that needs no further justification precisely because it is grounded in the nature of the self.

In their search for normative self-grounding, the later German idealists say a lot that can sound pretty unconvincing. For instance, take Fichte's notorious argument that "the not-I," everything outside the self, is in fact the product of "the I," or the self.[6] This way of talking makes it seem that Fichte is trying to say that the physical world, the world outside our own consciousness, is somehow the product of our own self-consciousness. If Fichte were really saying that, his position would be even more hopeless than Berkeley's: the Bishop had said that physical things were just ideas in our own minds, but even he didn't think that we had made them up ourselves. But if we think of Fichte as trying to show that Kant's proposed norms of theoretical reasoning are in fact self-grounded, his argument makes much

[5] Christine Korsgaard, *The Sources of Normativity* (Cambridge University Press, 1996).
[6] J. G. Fichte, *The Science of Knowledge*, ed. and trans. Peter Heath and John Lachs (Cambridge University Press, 2003). For a useful discussion of Fichte's relation to Hegel's response to Kant, see Robert Pippin, *Hegel's Idealism: The Satisfactions of Self-Consciousness* (Cambridge University Press, 1989), pp. 42–59.

more sense. Kant had said that our theoretical reasoning has to be empirical, because rationality requires that we appeal to standards that are available to everyone. Again, however, this argument presumes the value of public legislation, of appealing to everyone, as a normative ideal, and if we assume that this norm must be grounded in our nature as free and rational beings, then we need a further argument that shows that a free subject is somehow committed to this norm. And Fichte's argument is meant to accomplish just this. He argues that if free selves are to understand themselves as having identities as particular individuals, they can do so only if they can distinguish themselves as independent objects in the world, as one individual distinct from all the rest. A distinction between the "I" and the "not-I" is thus essential if the "I" is to understand itself as having a determinate identity. And this means that a free self must also recognize the independent existence of a physical world, which, as independent, can only be studied through the senses. Kant's norms of theoretical reason, and his ideal of understanding one's claims as publicly legislative, are thus understood as part of individuals' understanding themselves as individuals, as having particular identities.

Fichte clearly thought he was giving Kant's view a more stable grounding, but in fact there is an important difference between his kind of position and Kant's. The norms of modern scientific reasoning require a mechanistic account of the world; if your account of nature says anything about God's or anyone else's purposes or goals, you are not doing natural science any more. That includes your own goals as a scientific inquirer: even if they prompted you to do science, or a particular kind of science, if your own goals show up in your description of the natural world, what you are doing cannot count as science. Now Kant's account of scientific reasoning may be idealist, but it is not purposive or teleological. Kant did say that we impose the norms of science on the world, but he did not say anything about why it is that we do this, beyond the need to generate agreement – a goal that does not impose any individual's own purposes on any scientific description of the world. Indeed, Kant can tell a plausible story about why it is that scientific accounts of the world must be impersonal or mechanistic: if they were not, then their appeals to purposes would somehow have to cohere with each scientist's own interests or goals, a requirement that would hinder the goal of universal agreement. But by telling a further story about why the goal of universal agreement is important, Fichte begins to appeal to the sort of purposiveness that modern science is determined to exclude. On his view, the norms of scientific reasoning have their origin in each person's own goal of understanding himself or herself as a particular individual. This way of talking requires an explicit appeal to self-realization; while a Kantian can try to say that scientific norms reflect our identities as free agents, a Fichtean has to say that scientific norms help us realize those identities. And that suggests that the project of self-realization will be going on during scientific reasoning itself, which in turn suggests that the content of a scientific account will itself be affected by the project of self-realization. This is the reason that most contemporary analytic philosophers, who presume scientific naturalism from the start, are at least willing to listen to Kant, but don't see any point in listening to Fichte. And after Fichte there really is a good deal of German idealist and Romantic writing about natural science that is shot through with appeals to the purposiveness of nature. Today "organicism" – the sort of view that sees atoms or the cosmos as a whole as somehow analogous to living beings – is dismissed as crackpot science, but in the first part of the nineteenth century, it was taken quite seriously. Fichte himself may not have believed that the natural world cannot be understood without an appeal to self-realization or self-development, but in trying to ground Kant's theoretical norms in the self's coming to understand itself, he reopened the door to purposive or teleological views of nature.

The problem shows up again in the moral and political realms. Kant's account of practical norms is essentially liberal: he argues that the point of moral and political norms is not to realize any person's ends, but rather to allow all persons to pursue the ends that they have chosen for themselves, consistent with similar freedom for all others. Fichte accepts the whole of this account, except that by arguing that practical norms are grounded in an individual's project of self-realization, he again threatens to bring individuals' own purposes and goals into an area – this time, the norms of liberal morality and politics – from which they were supposed to be excluded.

Together, the notions of freedom and self-realization are dangerously destabilizing. Nietzsche later linked them together, but he also tends to celebrate destabilization, and especially the destabilization of the scientific and moral norms that Kant had wanted to defend. If you think that agents are free to choose their own projects, and you also think that the norms that govern the pursuit of those projects are grounded in the ability of those agents to realize themselves through the pursuit of those projects, then it looks like your account of normativity is explicitly subjective. Norms are essentially connected to an agent's goals, but since there are no goals that all free agents are presumed to share, norms seem to be just the imposition of some agent's goals on others. This is exactly what Nietzsche celebrates: the free and realized individual is one who imposes particular, novel, and in some sense arbitrary laws or standards on others. Nietzsche replies to Rousseau's challenge by reviving a version of Thrasymachus' position: since morality is imposed on us, the goal is to be the one doing the imposing. But since Nietzsche has a modern view of freedom, since he has read his Rousseau correctly, he isn't saying, like Thrasymachus, that you should seek power so that you can enjoy yourself all the time. As we have already seen, that way of thinking presumes that the social imposition of norms is only a means to a further, independent end. Like Rousseau, Nietzsche agrees that social imposition is really what matters. The difference is that Nietzsche argues, unconventionally but very cleverly, that the project of imposition, of being a form- or law-giving individual, is not a scandal to human freedom but rather its realization.

The impasse we have reached looks like this. If we take Rousseau's challenge seriously, we need to find a way of showing what Kant tried to show, that meaningful theoretical and practical norms are somehow grounded in the nature of human freedom. Kant's own arguments for this conclusion depended on a conception of free and rational persons as public legislators, as proposing claims that all could freely accept. Then the question is how to ground this commitment to public legislation in the nature of freedom. Why must a free and rational agent be committed to proposing only claims that all could freely accept? After Kant, in later German idealism, there is a tendency both to press hard on the notion of freedom, by asking this further question, and to propose substantive answers to the question that rely on some sort of notion of self-realization. But together, the notions of freedom and self-realization look dangerously subjective: it looks like individuals should just be able to do whatever they want, as long as they can justify the things they do as truly their own projects. By the time Hegel wrote the *Phenomenology*, it seemed to him that in their zealous efforts to justify Kant's position, Kant's idealist successors had in fact undermined any meaningful notion of justification. Kant had tried to reply to Rousseau by connecting rationality to freedom, and his followers had tried to defend his notion of freedom by finally detaching it from rationality.

HEGEL'S PROPOSED SOLUTION

It took Hegel a good deal of time to arrive at what he understood as a way out of this impasse. In the early stages of his philosophical career, Hegel tended to sidestep or dismiss the problems raised by Fichte's account rather than confronting them directly. In his first published work, *The Difference between Fichte's and Schelling's Systems of Philosophy* (1801), Hegel worked to defend his friend Schelling (and Hölderlin too) in the attempt to go beyond Fichte's subjectivism. Against Fichte, Hegel argued that the abstract notion of an "I," separated from the world and free to choose as it wished, led to a series of unresolved and irresolvable problems about how the subject could realize its essential nature through any engagement with the world. As he argued even more forcefully in his second book, *Faith and Knowledge* (1802), the problem was endemic to any philosophy of "reflection," by which Hegel meant any view that presumed a sharp separation between subject and object. In rejecting such separation, Hegel was following Schelling's argument that any actual subject is always already involved with the objects of the world.[7] Taken as the observation that any thought requires actual content, and that this content will always have some external component, this is a wholly unobjectionable point. However, for just that reason, it also doesn't provide any sort of answer to the question of what sort of content a subject ought to affirm, or in the language we have been using, what particular norms reflect our nature as free beings. That was the problem that Kant and Fichte were trying to address by emphasizing an independent subject in the first place, and to the extent that Schelling has a solution to this problem, it is just to romanticize his point about the subject's necessary involvement with its object. For Schelling, this point shows that there is a deep connection between the free subject and its world, that the realms of freedom and nature are ultimately united, despite all appearances. Philosophy's (and perhaps poetry's) job is then to bring out this connection, which Schelling calls "the Absolute" (a version of the German Romantic vision of unity discussed in Chapter 1). In his early work, we can say, Hegel saw that Fichte's position could lead to an unhappy form of subjectivism or skepticism, but he also thought, with Schelling, that Fichte's problem of normative self-grounding could be avoided from the start by appealing to some prior unity of subject and object, of freedom and external norms, that somehow underpins every act or thought of the subject.

By the time of the *Phenomenology*, though, Hegel came to regard this "solution" as simply dogmatic, as providing no meaningful guidance in distinguishing between self-grounded and arbitrarily imposed norms. Hence the *Phenomenology's* notorious characterization of the Absolute as "the night in which all cows are black" (16), a passage that makes no explicit mention of Schelling but that he and the rest of the German philosophical public

---

7 Schelling's position is most comprehensively defended in his *System of Transcendental Idealism*, ed. and trans. Peter Heath (University of Virginia Press, 1993).

understood as a direct and mocking attack. Together with the professional rivalry that intensified as Hegel overtook Schelling in philosophical reputation, this change of mind effectively ended the two men's friendship.

In one sense, however, this dispute was overblown, because despite this criticism of Schelling, Hegel never stopped believing that the solution to Fichte's problem was something called "the Absolute," and that it looked just like Schelling (and other German Romantics) had said it did: a kind of unity of the free subject with the world and with all other subjects. The difference, as Hegel announced at the start of the *Phenomenology* and continued to insist on throughout all of his later works, is that the Absolute must be conceived of not as any sort of preestablished harmony between ourselves and the world – which Hegel describes as "monotony and abstract universality" (16) – but only as "a result," the end of a process of historical development. "Of the Absolute it must be said that it is essentially a *result*, that only in the *end* is it what it truly is; and precisely in this consists its nature, viz. to be actual, subject, the spontaneous becoming of itself" (20). A free and realized individual, Hegel argued, is one who has emerged from such a process of historical development to achieve a kind of unity or identification with his or her social world and the norms that govern it. In this kind of unity, individuals understand themselves as free precisely because they conform to norms that reflect the value of the free individual. This realized condition, the Absolute, the end or goal of both philosophy and history, Hegel calls "Spirit's self-realization." To Rousseau's question of when and how human beings can be said to be free even as they live under social norms, Hegel's answer is: when Spirit has come to know itself.

At this point these formulations are so vague, so abstract, and so laden with new and seemingly fanciful terminology (besides "Spirit" and "the Absolute," Hegel also likes to speak of "the Notion" and "the Idea") that they are essentially meaningless (which is pretty much all of what many philosophers have thought there is to say about Hegel). But the *Phenomenology* is meant to provide a full defense of these formulations for a reader who is skeptical of everything that Hegel says. To that extent, our own examination of what Hegel means by "Spirit's knowledge of itself" must wait until the start of our discussion of the argument of the *Phenomenology* itself, in the next chapter. In the last pages of this chapter, I want only to clarify two crucial features of Hegel's position that should suggest the distinctiveness of his view of freedom. These clarifications will not provide any sort of defense of the view, but they should allow us to see where Hegel's view fits into the larger debates we have been exploring in this chapter: how Hegel's understanding of freedom does suggest a potential solution to the problems caused by Fichte's attempts to provide a deeper grounding for Kant's answer to Rousseau.

The two points I want to emphasize are these: first, that Hegel's view is that freedom is a kind of self-knowledge; and second, that this self-knowledge is the finished achievement of a process of self-exploration. In the context of post-Kantian idealism, and perhaps in the whole context of the modern discussion of freedom, the first view is unusual and even counterintuitive. For it seems clear that the notion of freedom is essentially practical, not theoretical: it refers primarily to actions and not to any sort of knowledge, of the self or of anything else. Obviously Hobbes' primary idea of physical freedom is a property of objects in motion. And even though his secondary idea of inner or moral freedom – the kind of freedom that is then emphasized as primary by Rousseau, Kant, and Fichte – is essentially a property of judgments rather than of physical movements, the idea of free judgment continues to refer to an active and not a contemplative state. For Kant, as we have now noted many times, to judge freely is to impose a kind of publicly legislative structure on the world. This emphasis on freedom as active legislation remains operative, in different forms, throughout the work of Kierkegaard and Nietzsche: to judge freely is to impose a particular shape on one's life. But for Hegel, to judge freely means to conclude that some norm reflects your own identity as an agent. In a sense, this is Kant's view too, except that for Kant, what it ultimately means for a norm to reflect your own identity is that you legislated the norm for yourself and all others. For Hegel, by contrast, all free acceptance means is that you identify with the norm. Still, you have to identify with it in the right way; not all identifications, and thus not all norms, count as freely accepted. But what Hegel means by free acceptance does not require any act of legislation: all it requires is that you can find a real coherence between your own history and the history of the norm, such that your identification with it makes rational sense. In this sense, Hegel's account is closer to Descartes' than to Kant's: the goal is to acquire a kind of knowledge of oneself, not to do anything in the world.

Still, it would seem that you could find this identification between your own history and the history of a norm without the norm's having a real justification; that there is a kind of rational coherence between you and the norm does not mean that you and the norm really are rational. For this reason, it is important to see that Hegel's second view, that the process of self-exploration unfolds over time, is meant to have real bite. Hegel is not just saying that self-knowledge can often take some time; he is saying that it necessarily takes time, that it can only occur at the end of a process of experience and self-discovery that is, in some sense, the project of every subject. In this sense, Hegel's account of self-knowledge is not at all like Descartes'. It is theoretical or contemplative, but what it contemplates is not the mind's own ideas, but rather the self's actual experiences in the world. The practical or active nature of the self, the point that was emphasized by Kant and then by Fichte, thus plays an essential role here: the self's actions and experiences are the material necessary for successful, retrospective understanding of oneself. What Hegel is saying is that every subject is committed to a kind of retrospective self-understanding, and that this commitment is in no sense optional. Assuming this is true, it then makes sense for Hegel to go on to argue that a truly rational identification of individuals with norms consists of both those individuals and those norms sharing not just any common history, but a particular common history, one in which both the individual and his or her culture became aware of their true nature as subjects: that is, as retrospective self-knowers. It is for this reason that Hegel begins to speak not just of the nature of subjectivity, but also of a kind of historical or collective subject, Spirit, that comes to full consciousness of itself over time. This does not mean that history or any community is somehow alive, despite what Hegel sometimes seems to say, but it does mean that Hegel believes we can say that individuals are really free only when they can authentically identify with collective norms, and that they can make this authentic identification only after a process of self-exploration that unfolds not just at the individual but also at the collective (i.e., the historical and cultural) level.

In what follows, then, I shall proceed under the assumption that Hegel's project in the *Phenomenology* is to vindicate this claim. That is, I will take it as Hegel's task to show that the essential nature of subjectivity, what it means to be a free and rational being, is not, as Kant thought, to actively engage in public legislation, but rather to engage in a process of retrospective self-discovery through reflection on one's own history. For now, though, what we need to understand about the claim is that it is meant to admit the concern with self-realization that allowed Fichte to attempt a deeper grounding for Kant's view of freedom, while at the same time avoiding the subjectivist or destabilizing consequences of Fichte's view.

Here it is crucial to emphasize that the concern with self-understanding is one that it seems safe to conclude that everyone can be taken to share. Fichte had already tried to exploit this very point: when thinking about the subject's imposition of the Kantian norms of theoretical or scientific reason, he argued that the positing of the "not-I" was essential if the "I" was to understand itself as an "I." The problem with this argument, as we have already seen, is that it looks like the "not-I" can be conceived of or structured to suit the "I"'s own purposes, which opens the door to both teleological natural science and a more general subjectivism. To avoid these consequences, Hegel denies vigorously that his subject is ever seeking to impose a structure or anything else on the world. The world, on his view, does not exist to serve the needs of the subject; it is merely the necessary field in which the subject's experiences unfold over time. Here again is Schelling's point that any subject is always already involved with the world, but it is important to see that Hegel does not understand this point as any sort of conclusion. Rather, the subject's essential involvement with the world is simply a precondition for the subject's later attempts to comprehend itself through a reflection on its experiences. Here it is crucial that the Hegelian project of self-understanding is always contemplative and retrospective; it only seeks to comprehend what has already occurred, not to change the world into something new. There is a project of self-realization here, one that is invoked to ground the justification of norms in the nature of the self, but since that project of self-realization is merely contemplative, it does not simply impose a subject's arbitrary rule on the world.

Since Rousseau, I have argued in this chapter, the philosophical problem of modern freedom has been to somehow reconcile the free judgments of the individual with the socially imposed judgments of collective norms. The most important solution to this problem was Kant's claim that we should see justified norms as the product of the individual's own commitment to public legislation. Then the problem became to ground this commitment to public legislation in the self's own nature, without simply celebrating the freedom of the individual to impose any structure it wants on the world. Hegel's own response is to abandon the legislative or form-giving conception of freedom for an alternative, contemplative picture of freedom of judgment as grounded in retrospective self-understanding. Now the problem is to give this new picture of the subject and its freedom a philosophical defense.

CHAPTER 5

Method

The central principle of his philosophy, Hegel announces at the start of the *Phenomenology*, is that of subjectivity. "In my view, which can be justified only by the exposition of the system itself, everything turns on grasping and expressing the True, not only as *Substance*, but equally as *Subject*" (17). Notice the double task: to grasp and to express. This means, first, that the goal of philosophical inquiry must be conceived of as an inquiry into the nature of subjectivity. But it also means, second, that philosophical inquiry must simultaneously take the form of subjectivity, exhibiting the nature of subjectivity itself. The object of philosophical inquiry is now the subject, but for this very reason, philosophical inquiry cannot stand about from its object in a traditional contemplative stance. For this would undermine the Hegelian claim that philosophy is concerned with the subject and not with objects external to the subject. Rather, philosophy must be simply the expression of the subject itself. But what kind of expression? What exactly is the subject, and how must its nature be manifested in philosophy itself?

CONTEMPLATIVE AND ACTIVE SUBJECTIVITY

We have already seen that the concern with subjectivity is not new: it is a dominant theme of modern philosophy from Descartes to Kant. But Hegel thinks that only his philosophy can rid this tradition of its incoherencies and misunderstandings. More specifically, Hegel's claim is that only his conception of subjectivity can make sense of the two distinctive features of subjectivity emphasized by modern philosophy, rendering them consistent with both each other and themselves.

These two features of subjectivity are those respectively emphasized by Descartes and then by Kant:

1. For Descartes, subjectivity is primarily a contemplative starting point, chosen to ensure methodological certainty. I cannot be sure that what I am thinking corresponds to reality, but I can be sure that I am thinking,

and thinking these particular thoughts. By staying within the realm of my thoughts, then, and examining them only as thoughts, I cannot go wrong. The problem, of course, is how to transfer the logical connections between my thoughts, the relations of my ideas, to claims about the physical world. Ultimately Cartesian rationalism could not justify its claims about the world beyond the self without a dogmatic theological premise, a claim that there simply must be a God with whose help (as in Descartes himself) or from whose nature (as in Spinoza and Leibniz) we could deduce the logical/physical structure of the world. Cartesian subjectivity is meant to guarantee the strict necessity appropriate to philosophy, but its posture of self-contemplation lacks any necessary connection to the world of objects.

2. As we saw in Chapter 2, this rationalist account of science (which is still present in Locke's wish to find the real essences of substances) was gradually undermined by the criticism and self-criticism of the empiricist tradition, and especially by Hume's skepticism about the rationality of our causal beliefs. Confronted with Hume's conclusion that none of our concepts is the source of rational necessity, that our claims to necessity in fact arise from the contingent effects of our experiences, Kant tried to reestablish the objectivity of both empirical knowledge and moral principles through a second, quite different appeal to subjectivity. For transcendental idealism, we can have scientific knowledge of the world because, at bottom, the physical/causal structure of nature can be traced back to the structure of our own mental faculties. Kant's methodological principle seems to be the same as Descartes': in knowing the world, we never really leave our own thoughts, our own representations. We can rely on our causal claims because causality is part of our conceptual apparatus, built into any conception we might have of an object. But ultimately the Kantian conception of subjectivity is not a contemplative one. Rather, contemplation of objects (including self-contemplation) is possible only because the subject is originally active, imprinting a physical/causal structure onto the world. Ultimately the world is what it is and must be for us because we make it so. What the world would be like without our activity we simply cannot say.

This second, idealist conception of subjectivity is thus a radically active or spontaneous one. Kantian, transcendental subjectivity points beyond the theoretical contemplation of objects, and beyond Cartesian introspection, toward an active, form-giving self. And in fact the whole of Kant's critical philosophy is structured to legitimate this transition from a theoretical to a practical conception of the self. For Kant, reason is a fundamentally active and creative faculty, constructing Ideas that go beyond anything given in experience. Through a process of criticism or self-discipline, reason learns to restrict its claims about the world to claims about objects of possible experience. But this process of self-limitation itself clears the way for reason's self-assertion in the practical or moral realm. The Idea of freedom has no application in the realm of knowledge, since it corresponds to nothing we experience in the empirical world. But for this very reason, we cannot say that the Idea of freedom has no reality: all we can say is that freedom cannot become an object of knowledge for us. Hence there is room for Kant to assert that from another, purely practical point of view, we can understand ourselves as free. This point of view, Kant thinks, is already presupposed in ordinary moral experience and is already justified by our sense of ourselves as moral and hence rational beings.

Kant's position, then, can be summarized as follows: the theoretical contemplation of objects itself presupposes the conception of free, active subjectivity that finds its full expression in the moral/practical realm. In contrast to Descartes, there is no special problem here about how to move from the inner realm of the subject to the external world of objects. For it is the essential nature of the Kantian subject to shape the world of objects to its own subjective form. But there is now a special problem about specifying the nature of the Kantian subject's activity. If the subject is defined as fundamentally spontaneous or free, why does it choose one form of activity over another? Kant says that the theoretical self shapes the world of objects into physical/causal form, according to the twelve categories of understanding. But why these categories and not others? Kant then says that the practical self constrains itself according to a principle of universalizability, to the dictates of the moral law. But why the moral law, and why this conception of the moral law?

In Chapter 4, I emphasized that Kant attempts to answer these questions by grounding the norms of science and morality in the subject's commitment to public legislation, of proposing claims that all others could accept. But what justifies the claim that the free subject is essentially committed to the ideal of public legislation? Any answer to this deeper question faces a dilemma – a dilemma that Hegel thinks neither Kant nor his German idealist successors were able to overcome. If the Kantian subject chooses to confine itself to a particular form of activity, it seems to be denying its own nature as a free and spontaneous being. For such a being is precisely one that is free of external constraints. But if the Kantian subject rejects any constraint as hostile to its nature, it seems to have no reason for choosing one form of activity over another. All such a subject can do is arbitrarily assert itself, either by lashing out at whatever form of constraint seems to be in its vicinity, or perhaps by arbitrarily celebrating its intuitive sense of its own sublime nature:

> But just as there is an empty breadth, so there is an empty depth, and just as there is an extension of substance that pours forth as a finite multiplicity without the force to hold the multiplicity together, so there is an intensity without content, one that holds itself in as a sheer force without spread, and this is in no way distinguishable from superficiality. The power of Spirit is only as great as its expression, its depth only as deep as it dares to spread out and lose itself in its exposition. Moreover, when this non-conceptual, substantial knowledge professes to have sunk the idiosyncrasy of the self in essential being, and to philosophize in a true and holy manner, it hides the truth from itself: by spurning measure and definition, instead of being devoted to God, it merely gives free rein both to the contingency of the content within it, and to its own caprice. (10)

In both the destructive fury of the French Revolution and in Romanticism's celebration of our spiritual powers, Hegel saw the arbitrary force of the free subject unleashed from any constraints other than the strength of its own convictions. Kant had hoped that his free and spontaneous subject would confine itself to the orderly and productive realms of science and morality. But there seems no reason to believe that a free subject has any reason for necessarily choosing these particular forms of activity. Unless we can show what a free subject would necessarily choose, the Kantian conception of subjectivity looks irrational, arbitrary, and perhaps even dangerous. While the Cartesian conception of subjectivity is locked within itself, unable to apply its methodological self-certainty to the world, the Kantian conception is left to roam aimlessly about the world, unable to justify its self-assertion in any rational way.

Hegel's response to this impasse is to opt for the Kantian conception of subjectivity, but to try to rescue it with a Cartesian twist. The subject, Hegel agrees with Kant, is fundamentally an active and creative force that ought to be bound by no external constraint. But what then does the subject do, beyond overturning all such constraints? Hegel's answer is: nothing but realize the error of its ways. The subject's fundamental nature is simply to overturn all external constraints, and then to realize that this is a futile and irrational activity. But in recognizing this, the subject gains a kind of knowledge of itself. The subject realizes that it has foolishly tried to assert itself against every form of constraint – precisely to achieve a sense of itself as active. And in understanding its actions in this way, the subject gains, finally, an accurate sense of itself – a sense that it would never have had without its seemingly fruitless attempt at revolt. What is in one sense a process of arbitrary self-assertion comes to be understood, retrospectively, as a kind of journey to self-knowledge.

In the Preface to the *Phenomenology*, Hegel describes the subject's struggle with and against the constraints on its freedom in the most dramatic terms: as a struggle with and against death. Death, Hegel says, consists in "non-actuality" (32), and in a sense, the freedom of the subject is the power to inflict death, because the freedom of the subject is the power to reject the claims of any existing person or any existing standard of action as inconsistent with its freedom. "But that an accident as such, detached from what circumscribes it, what is bound and actual only in its context with others, should attain an existence of its own and a separate freedom – this is the tremendous power of the negative, it is the energy of thought, of the pure 'I'" (32). But the death that the free subject risks in its struggle with external constraints is in fact its own, because the world of other people and actual social norms is what gives life and reality to any living person; it provides the real and meaningful content of a person's life. This is the lesson that the free subject learns in its struggle against the standards that constrain it:

But the life of Spirit is not the life that shrinks from death and keeps itself untouched by devastation, but rather the life that endures it and maintains itself in it. It wins its truth only when, in utter dismemberment, it finds itself. It is this power, not as something positive, which closes its eyes to the negative, as when we say of something that it is nothing or is false, and then, having done with it, turn away and pass on to something else; on the contrary, Spirit is this power only by looking the negative in the face, and tarrying with it. This tarrying with the negative is the magical power that converts it into being. (32)

In this struggle with death, the free subject learns that what seemed to be opposed to its nature as free – the external forces that seem to limit and constrain its nature – turn out to be essential to its true nature, which is to understand itself, retrospectively, as the product of this very struggle. This, Hegel says in the most sweeping of terms, is the deepest insight of philosophy, the Idea that governs all rational thought. "*Pure* self-recognition in absolute otherness, this Aether *as such*, is the ground and soil of Science or *knowledge in general*" (26). At times, particularly in crude interpretations of Hegel, this very general emphasis on the reconciliation of opposites, on unity within difference, is seen as a basic logical or conceptual truth that governs the operation of everything in the world. Hegel does in fact entitle his systematic philosophical account of this Idea the *Logic*, and some of his descriptions of natural science do make it sound as if he regards the unity of opposites as some kind of deeper law of physics. But there is no reason that Hegel should be read in this way; he is clear in all his works, including the *Logic*, that self-recognition in otherness is a property not of concepts or of nature, but rather of subjects and their attempts to understand themselves.

In the background here is a kind of insight that we might first identify as sociological or psychological. Hegel is describing what ought to seem familiar to us as a process of human development, a path through which an individual reaches maturity. At the beginning of this path, in childhood, there is a kind of unreflective dependence on the thoughts and wishes of others. But the maturing individual must ultimately reject this kind of unreflective dependence if her actions and choices are to be understood as her own. This rejection, in what we might call a kind of adolescence, may well take the form of a revolt against her family's or community's standards and values. Such a revolt, however, is as much a confession of dependence as it is an attempt at self-assertion. For the rejection of the familiar values is, in fact, arbitrary, justified only by the contingent presence of the rejected values. One cannot free oneself from the arbitrary rule of a parent by simply adopting the negation of the parent's commands. Ultimately this sort of revolt is merely a revolt against the idea of standards and values – a revolt that is itself both incoherent and immature. But it may be that this sort of failed revolt is a necessary stage on the way to full maturity, a situation in which an individual chooses for herself without simply lashing out against all existing social norms.

By reconceiving the subject's activity as a project of self-realization or self-development, Hegel thus seeks to combine the best features of the Cartesian and the Kantian accounts of subjectivity. The Hegelian subject is a fundamentally active subject, fully engaged with the world as it struggles to overcome the constraints of existing yet arbitrary social norms. But its activity is fundamentally its own, since its goal is always a kind of self-knowledge, a sense of its own identity within the world. It achieves this identity through a journey to self-knowledge that is at the same time a process of winning its freedom through its own activity.

THE FREE SUBJECT AND ITS CULTURE

At the end of this process, it would seem that we still have the problem: what standards or values, what form of social life, would a chastened, mature Hegelian subject accept? Once the subject's arbitrary revolt against all external standards is concluded, once this subject agrees to return to the mundane world of existing social practices, what sort of life makes rational sense?

The short Hegelian answer to this question is: those social practices that are themselves committed to the value of the free and active subject. But that answer looks empty, because it seems to return us to the original, Kantian problem: what actual content can be given to the abstract notion of freedom? At the individual level, Hegel wants to solve this problem by describing freedom as a process of self-assertion and then of self-knowledge: first a revolt against existing social norms, and then a reconciliation to the idea of such norms. But because this journey of the free subject must end in a return to social life, Hegel is again left to provide content for the notion of freedom, this time at the communal or social level. And here it would seem that the Hegelian account of freedom as a journey to self-knowledge is of little help. But in fact Hegel thinks this account is all that he needs, because he thinks that he can apply it at the social or communal level as well. That is, Hegel thinks he can describe the history of modern Western societies as a process analogous to the individual's journey to self-development. "The task of leading the individual from his uneducated standpoint to knowledge had to be seen in its universal sense, just as it was the universal self-conscious Spirit, whose formative education had to be studied" (28). The social practices that are committed to the value of the free subject are precisely those that have emerged from this kind of historical process.

It is at this point that Hegel's account begins to look bizarre, because he is willing to describe Western history as the journey to self-knowledge of a kind of collective, historical subject, which he calls Spirit (*Geist*). It seems as if Hegel is invoking the presence of some sweeping cosmic entity, unknown to empirical science yet somehow much more important and influential than any physical force. But there is neither physical nor metaphysical out- landishness here, if we understand Spirit simply as what a particular form of social life, a particular social practice, takes to be its most important standards of value. These standards of value, of course, have no existence outside the beliefs and intentions of the individuals who are committed to them. But because the individuals who are committed to social norms do not choose them abstractly, outside the context of already existing social practices, we can coherently speak of both norms and practices as having a kind of independent existence, helping to socialize individuals and to orient them in their choices. Hence when some particular group of individuals, engaging in some particular social practice, understands some norm under- lying that social practice as a shared, important, and worthy standard of value, we can say, with Hegel, that Spirit has taken on a particular shape.

Still, why invoke Spirit if one can just as easily speak of practices, norms, and values? What good does this terminology do Hegel or anybody else? Here we must remember that Hegel is talking not just about practices, norms, and values but also about the processes through which they develop and change. Even more crucially, Hegel is talking about the ways in which these cultural developments and changes can be understood as more (or less) rational. Because Spirit refers specifically to those norms that individuals in a particular culture understand as shared, important, and worthy, the individuals affirming the particular norms need to be able to give a rational account of what gives the norms their importance and their worth. Hegel's deeper claim is that such a rational account is just a historical story that describes how the norm came to be affirmed in that particular culture – a story that itself traces the pattern of self-realization we have already described. The values and norms of the modern West, Hegel is saying, can be rationally defended as valuable precisely because they emerged from a historical process in which Western culture rejected the idea of existing norms and values as externally imposed, and then came to see this rejection as itself misguided.

This collective, historical process gets its claim to rationality through its analogy with the individual's own struggle for freedom: "... regarded from the side of universal Spirit as substance, this is nothing but its own acquisition of self-consciousness, the bringing-about of its own becoming and reflection into itself" (28). It is for this reason that Hegel can and must speak of a collective subject called Spirit, and not simply of social practices, norms, and values. Without the analogy to the individual subject, Hegel's position would collapse into an exceedingly weak form of historicism or communitarianism. According to this weak view – much associated with Hegel but most assuredly not his – there are no standards of rationality except those that are internal to particular social practices, such that there is no rational basis for criticizing other social practices on external grounds. Hegel accepts the historicist premise of this view, but he emphatically rejects the relativism that might seem to follow from it. The idea of free, self-realizing subjectivity is in fact a historically grounded standard of value, emerging in Western history at a particular time. But it carries a trans-historical claim to rationality that seeks to defend the practices, norms, and values of the modern West as rationally superior to those of other actual and potential cultures. This trans-historical claim to rationality is just what is asserted by Hegel's describing the cultural and political life of the modern West as the self-realization of Spirit. What this means is that the practices, norms, and values of the modern West themselves have emerged from a historical process that traces the pattern and reflects the value of self-realizing subjectivity.

Now the crucial question becomes: where does the idea of self-realizing subjectivity get its claim to rationality? From the philosophical point of view – the point of view explicitly concerned with the nature and power of rationality – everything we have said so far has the status of mere assertion. We have defended the coherence of the Hegelian conception of subjectivity, but we have given it no philosophical justification of any kind.

Specifically, we have said that the Hegelian conception of subjectivity overcomes the defects and combines the best features of the Cartesian and Kantian accounts of subjectivity. But why care about the internal weaknesses of these previous accounts? If they are inadequate, why not abandon the modern concern with subjectivity entirely, as "common sense" philosophers like Thomas Reid had already suggested?

We have then described Hegelian self-realizing subjectivity as a process of maturation that we are likely to find familiar from our experience of human social life. But this seems at best a weak empirical claim about human nature or, more likely, about human nature as it manifests itself in certain forms of society. Even if the claim is coherent, it hardly seems to carry the sort of strict necessity to which Descartes and Kant aspired. Why should we regard Hegel's account of self-development as a philosophical claim, particularly if we are committed to a more traditional conception of philosophy that rejects the modern concern with subjectivity in favor of the theoretical contemplation of objects? Why does Hegel think he has grasped not just a contingent feature of some human subjects, but the essential nature of subjectivity itself? And what can he say to those who understand the task of philosophy as concerned with substance rather than with the subject?

Things look even bleaker when we recall Hegel's aspiration not just to grasp the essential nature of subjectivity, but also to express that nature in his philosophical work. So as to treat the subject as not simply another object, Hegel demands that his work take the form of a subject's journey to self-knowledge. Thus he conceives of his philosophical project not as a traditional treatise of any sort, but as a kind of fictionalized autobiography of his collective subject, Spirit. We have defended the idea of Spirit as coherent, and we have seen why Hegel wants and needs to invoke it. But why must anyone else feel compelled to invoke the notion of Spirit? And how will they be convinced by a philosophical work that already assumes that philosophy is itself nothing other than the self-realization of Spirit?

Hegel faces what seems to be an intractable dilemma of justification. He is trying to undermine a more traditional conception of philosophy in which we seek to understand the fundamental nature of the objects that are external to the subject. In place of this theoretical or contemplative sort of philosophy, Hegel wants to substitute a new concern with active, self-realizing subjectivity. Without an argument for this new conception of philosophy, Hegel's claims will have the status of mere assertion. But how can he argue for a Hegelian conception of philosophy? If he argues in his opponents' theoretical terms, his argument will be self-undermining: it will presuppose the very conception of philosophical argument Hegel is trying to overcome. But if he argues in his own, Hegelian terms, his argument will seem to be question-begging: it will not convince anyone committed to the more traditional conception of philosophical justification.

Hegel's response to this dilemma is a characteristic one: he argues that it is not really a dilemma at all. We can have it both ways: we can argue convincingly against the traditional conception of philosophy yet assume the Hegelian conception all along. We can do this if we adopt a method of skepticism, while nonetheless coming to understand the destructive path of skeptical argument as finally productive of subjectivity itself.

For purposes of justification, we begin with the traditional conception of philosophy and examine it in its own, theoretical terms. When we do this, Hegel claims, we will see that this conception is beset with a series of skeptical doubts, doubts that it is unable to overcome without assuming Hegel's own account of subjectivity. In trying to justify itself, the theoretical conception of philosophy will finally collapse into the Hegelian conception.

Natural consciousness will show itself to be only the Notion of knowledge, or in other words, not to be real knowledge. But since it directly takes itself to be real knowledge, this path has a negative significance for it, and what is in fact the realization of the notion, counts for it as the loss of its own self; for it does lose the truth on this path. The road can therefore be regarded as the pathway of *doubt,* or more precisely as the way of despair (78).

This might seem to constitute a purely theoretical and hence self-undermining argument for Hegelian subjectivity. But this is not necessarily the case – provided that we can come to see the process of skeptical doubt, and of overcoming that doubt, as itself reflecting the movement of Hegelian subjectivity. What seem to be merely the bumbling mistakes of the theoretical self may turn out to be, on further reflection, the necessary unfolding of the free, self-realizing subject.

To make this more intelligible, it may be remarked, in a preliminary and general way, that the exposition of the untrue consciousness in its untruth is not a merely *negative* procedure. The natural consciousness itself normally takes this one-sided view of it... This is just the skepticism which only ever sees pure nothingness in its result and abstracts from the fact that this nothingness is specifically the nothingness of that *from which it results*... But when, on the other hand, the result is conceived as in its truth, as a determinate negation, a new form has thereby immediately arisen, and in the negation the transition is made through which the progress through the complete series of forms comes about of itself. (79)

This second understanding is possible because Hegelian subjectivity is both (1) self-denying and then (2) retrospectively self-knowing. According to Hegel's account, we have seen, the subject is the sort of being that lashes out against standards of value external to itself, and that then comes to understand this revolt as futile and misguided. In the second stage of this process, what first seems external to the subject – the field of socially and historically given standards and practices – comes to be understood as essential to the subject's own identity. And this means that the first stage of the process of self-realization turns out, in hindsight, to count as a kind of self-denial – a self-denial that was itself a necessary part of self-development. It is in the Hegelian subject's essential nature to deny itself, and then retrospectively to understand the error of its ways.

But the goal is necessarily fixed for knowledge as the serial progression; it is the point where knowledge no longer needs to go beyond itself, where knowledge finds itself, where Notion corresponds to object and object to Notion. Hence the progress towards this goal is also unhalting, and short of it no satisfaction is to be found at any of the stations on the way. Whatever is confined within the limits of a natural life cannot by its own efforts go beyond its immediate existence; but it is driven beyond it by something else, and this uprooting entails its death. Consciousness, however, is explicitly the Notion of itself. Hence it is something that goes beyond limits, and since these limits are its own, it is something that goes beyond itself. With the positing of a single particular the beyond is also established for consciousness, even if it is only *alongside* the limited object as in the case of spatial intuition. Thus consciousness suffers violence at its own hands; it spoils its own limited satisfaction. When consciousness feels this violence, its anxiety may well make it retreat from the truth, and strive to hold on to what it is in danger of losing. But it can find no peace. (80)

Because the essential nature of consciousness, of the thinking subject, is to cast doubt on the particular thoughts that constitute the content of consciousness itself, the purely theoretical starting point of Hegel's skeptical philosophical method is in no sense self-undermining. Since the subject is essentially self-denying, we would have to expect a philosophical journey that expresses the nature of subjectivity to start with an act of self-denial: a claim that subjectivity itself is of no importance. We must thus start with the most purely theoretical standpoint possible: a standpoint that makes no reference to the subject, that assumes nothing but the nature of the objects of the world. If this theoretical standpoint tends to crumble under its own theoretical commitments, that is not only what a Hegelian, subjective conception of philosophy would demand; it is also an expression of the Hegelian conception itself.

In the progress of this skeptical argument, we assume only one value, the value internal to Western philosophy itself. This is the value of rational justification: the demand that any person articulate and defend his or her own standards and practices on grounds intelligible to any competent person. This is what Socrates demanded of his interlocutors, and it is all Hegel demands of the conceptions of philosophy that are opposed to his own. In this kind of examination, there is no need for an external "criterion" (83–85) which would have to correctly measure the contents of consciousness against the reality of the world. There is simply the internal test of consciousness' being able to express itself. Of course, Hegel's own view is that the philosophical demand for reasons is, at bottom, the expression of the subject's own active, self-realizing nature, against which it measures all particular forms of thought. But this is not something we assume from the start. Instead we assume just the opposite: that we can achieve a conception of the world free of any reference to subjectivity. We then, like Socrates, ask this conception of the world to articulate what it takes to be true. When these attempts at self-articulation fail, as Hegel thinks they do, we have not just an argument for a Hegelian, subjective conception of philosophy, but also, in hindsight, an expression of subjectivity's own attempt to know itself. The results of philosophical, skeptical pressure are not simply destructive or Socratically aporetic. Rather, they are productive of subjectivity itself – since, on Hegel's account, the subject is the sort of being that has to deny its own nature in order to understand itself as a subject. In this way, philosophy converts its Socratic aspiration, the love of knowing, into actual knowing (5): subjectivity's knowledge of itself.

PHILOSOPHY AS RETROSPECTIVE

Philosophy's special concern with rational justification and subjectivity's self-realizing nature are ultimately one and the same. Hegel can make this claim because he understands both the philosopher's demand for reasons and the subject's conception of its own free and active nature as fundamentally retrospective. What both the philosopher and the active subject are seeking is only available in hindsight, in a reconstructive account of what has already unfolded in the world.

For the subject, the task is to achieve a sense of its own freedom, a sense of itself as an active being. This sense of freedom is first sought in an arbitrary rejection of existing social norms. But since this revolt turns out to be irrational and immature, the free subject returns, chastened, to the shared and concrete world of social practices. But it can experience the return to this world of social practices as rational if it can understand those practices as reflecting its own process of adolescent revolt and chastened maturity. The individual subject can achieve this understanding if the history of its social practices, the coming to be of its cultural life, can be understood as analogous to the self-development of the individual. There is a double retrospection here – the individual looking back on her own history, and then the individual looking back on her community's history – with both forms of retrospection converging on the same pattern. The subject knows itself by looking back on its own activity, and it is able to rest content with this knowledge by looking back on its community's history and recognizing its own struggle there.

For the philosopher, the task is to justify our practices and our beliefs, to understand them as expressions of rationality. We do this by applying a thoroughgoing skepticism to our particular understandings of the world, by demanding of ourselves that we articulate and defend our implicit and as yet unexamined commitments. The results of this skeptical inquiry are, predictably enough, a rubble of discarded practices and beliefs. Philosophy has little to show for itself unless it can extract something positive from the casualties of its skeptical onslaught. But this something must be more than those practices and beliefs that survive skeptical challenge. For these would be nothing more than what we began with, unless we can show that we are better off for having gone through the process of philosophical criticism. To show that, to vindicate the philosophical process in philosophy's own terms, we must be able to show not just that there is something positive that survives philosophical skepticism, but also that this something could never have been what it is for us now had it not gone through the pro-cess of skeptical challenge. Philosophy's job, then, is to vindicate itself by describing its own destructive efforts as necessary for our current beliefs and practices. And this is something that can be achieved only in retrospect: by redescribing the history of philosophy not simply as a series of critical overturnings, but rather as a necessary process through which we came to our current ways of thinking.

In a sense, then, Hegel's position can be described quite simply. The Hegelian conception of subjectivity is the unique candidate for the object of philosophical inquiry itself. And this is true not simply because Hegel thinks he can show that it is this conception of subjectivity that can survive skeptical challenge (since understandings of the world that attempt to do without it cannot manage to articulate themselves). Rather, the Hegelian conception of subjectivity is the unique candidate for the object of philosophical inquiry because this conception of subjectivity would not be what it is for us without our having undergone the experience of the skeptical challenge. Because the Hegelian subject must undergo a long process of self-denial to come, retrospectively, to a knowledge of itself, it is uniquely suited to the needs of philosophy, which must also come to understand, retrospectively, the necessity of its own skeptical destruction. The subject's own attempt to understand itself as rational is finally what is and must be reason's own subject, the object of philosophical inquiry itself.

STAGES OF THE ARGUMENT

All of this, of course, must now be demonstrated in the actual progress of the skeptical or philosophical argument. In accordance with what we have said here, we should understand this argument as taking place in four stages, stages that determine the structure of the *Phenomenology of Spirit.*

1. In the first stage (corresponding to Hegel's chapter on "Consciousness" and to this book's Chapter 6), we begin with a purely theoretical conception of the world, purged of any reference to subjectivity of Hegel's or any other kind. We then show that this conception lapses into incoherence when it tries to articulate its claims about the world. From this we may conclude that the theoretical outlook would not be possible unless it presupposed a conception of subjectivity.

2. In the second stage of the argument (corresponding to Hegel's chapter on "Self-Consciousness" and to this book's Chapter 7), we begin with what might be called an isolated conception of subjectivity, purged of any reference to the shared practices, norms, and values that Hegel thinks are essential to any mature, realized subject. We then show that this bare conception of subjectivity lapses into incoherence, that this isolated subject cannot articulate its own conception of itself as independent while denying the relevance of social or cultural standards.

3. In the third stage of the argument (corresponding to Hegel's chapters on "Reason," "Spirit," and "Religion" and to this book's Chapter 8), we turn to the history of Western culture itself, looking for those shared standards

and practices that have shaped our theoretical and then our practical conceptions. What we find when we reconstruct this historical development is
a collective or shared history that is itself analogous to the journey of the
individual subject.

4. Finally, in the fourth stage of the argument (corresponding to Hegel's
chapter on "Absolute Knowing" and to this book's Chapter 9), we come to
understand, retrospectively, the connection between the philosophical or
skeptical justification of the first two stages of argument and the cultural
history of the third stage. We understand the philosophically vindicated
conception of subjectivity as not fully rational without an account of the
subject's history, and we understand such an account of history as not
fully rational unless it points to the conception of subjectivity itself. For
Hegel, the moment of reconciliation between these stages of argument is
symbolized in the Christian religion, and fully expressed in the successful
enterprise of philosophy itself.

CHAPTER 6

Theory

We have seen that Hegel's philosophical project is to vindicate a particular conception of subjectivity, and to demonstrate its essential connection to the idea of rational justification itself. To make this argument convincing, however, Hegel must not presuppose this conception of subjectivity. Rather he must consider and eliminate the possibility that there could be a rational conception of the world that does without it. And in fact a traditional aspiration of philosophy is to achieve a conception of the world that does without subjectivity of any kind. To know something, on this traditional view, is simply to know it as it is in itself, without any contribution from us. Call this a purely theoretical view of knowledge: to know the world as it truly is, we must stand apart from the world, in an entirely disinterested or contemplative posture.

Hegel's own view, of course, is that this view of knowledge is incoherent: were we to assume a purely theoretical standpoint, we could never achieve anything that we would count as knowledge. To show this, we subject the purely theoretical standpoint to skeptical critique. We imagine a person committed to the purely theoretical standpoint, and ask her how she might defend her beliefs as true.

SENSE-CERTAINTY

What would a purely theoretical view of the world look like? Hegel argues that we must begin with the theoretical aspiration in its simplest and most radical form. According to the pure theorist, we must eliminate anything in our account of an object that comes not from the object but from ourselves. We must rid ourselves of all our preconceptions, all our prior schemes of categorization, and attend only to the object itself. And we must attend to the object only in its purest and most unmediated form. So as not to distort the object, we must make ourselves entirely passive or receptive, allowing the object to impress its nature on us but not contributing anything ourselves:

77

"In *ap*prehending it, we must refrain from trying to *com*prehend it" (90). We must become the pure perceivers of traditional empiricism, attending only to what Locke called "simple ideas" and Hume called "impressions." If we can do this, we might achieve what Hegel calls sense-certainty.

In sense-certainty, we attend to an object without imposing anything on that object. We simply experience the object; to do anything more would be to risk distorting it with our preconceptions, judgments, and interests. To rid our thinking of its subjective element, that which is contributed by us, we must focus only on what the object immediately presents to us: sights, sounds, smells, touches, and tastes. By breaking down our thoughts of objects back into these simple, sensory components, we can achieve an undistorted view of the world. We will escape what Hobbes, Locke, and Hume warned us against: the abstractions and confusions that centuries of human language have placed between us and the world.

By experiencing the object in its immediacy, I seek to know it as it is in itself. But what do I know? I can say: I see the apple. But do I really see the apple? The word *apple* does not itself describe a sensory experience. Rather, it seems to stand for a range of possible sensory experiences: redness, roundness, tartness, and so on. In Locke's terminology, "apple" is a complex idea, composed of several simple ideas, each of which refers to a discrete sensory episode. To speak truly, then, I should not say, "I see the apple." Rather I should say, "I see the red, (nearly) round, shiny object," or even better, "I am experiencing certain visual sensations: redness, roundness, shininess."

But even this way of speaking is imprecise. Let's focus on just one of the reports of my sensory experience: "I see red." The word *red*, however, is not itself a report of a sensory experience; it is, once again, a universal term that applies to a range of possible sensory experiences. To speak truly, then, I cannot say "I see red" or "I am experiencing a sensation of redness." All I can say is that I am seeing this particular shade of red at this particular time. But even this description misses the particularity of my experience; by referring even to a "shade of redness," I implicitly invoke my other experiences and conceptions of red objects. In this way, I distort what I mean, which is to point to my current experience, and to my current experience only. Indeed, to preserve my meaning, all I can do is point, to say "This!," in the hope that others will look and experience the same sensation, that they too will see the particular shade of red that I am now seeing. But even this bare demonstrative does not capture what sense-certainty is trying to say:

It is, then, sense-certainty itself that must be asked: "What is the *This*?" If we take the "This" in the twofold shape of its being, as "Now" and as "Here," the dialectic it has in it will receive a form as intelligible as the "This" itself is. To the question:

"What is Now?," let us answer, e.g. "Now is Night." In order to test the truth of this sense-certainty a simple experiment will suffice. We write down this truth; a truth cannot lose anything by being written down, any more than it can lose anything through our preserving it. If *now, this noon*, we look again at the written truth we shall have to say that it has become stale. (95)

The same will be the case with the other form of the "This," with "Here." "Here" is, e.g., the tree. If I turn round, this truth has vanished and is converted into its opposite: "No tree is here, but a house instead." "Here" itself does not vanish; on the contrary, it abides constant in the vanishing of the house, the tree, etc., and is indifferently house or tree. Again, therefore, the "This" shows itself to be a *mediated simplicity*, or a *universality*. (98)

The "Here" and the "Now" are meant to pick out the specificity of my experience; they are supposed to point to the spatial and temporal location where it is available for others to experience as well. But in the saying of the "Here" and the "Now," the presence of my experience is lost. The other person may see the redness of the apple, but she does not see what I was experiencing at the moment of my utterance.

This may seem an absurd point to stress, but it is important to see that the stress, and thus the absurdity, come from the logic of sense-certainty itself. The goal of sense-certainty, of classical empiricism, is to break down our understandings of the world into absolutely simple and undistorted components. These components are simply experiences as they are in themselves. But an "experience" is a moment of pure presence; once it is described or even pointed to, it is no longer an experience in sense-certainty's pure sense. Of course we can share experiences; we can each see the same shade of red. But this is because we share a vocabulary, a stock of linguistic terms, in which to describe our experiences. Even if I merely point, even if I say only "This!," I can succeed in communicating my experience only if the other person attends to the same piece of experience that I did. And this, like any use of language, is already an exercise in abstraction: the other person picks out the feature of her experience that she assumes I must have picked out also. And to distinguish a feature of our experience is already to conceptualize it, to describe it in terms that can and must apply to a whole range of similar experiences. As soon as I succeed in communicating my sense of the object, then, I have destroyed the immediacy, the pure presence, that sense-certainty insisted was our best guide to an accurate and undistorted sense of the world.[1]

---

[1] For further discussion of this argument, see Charles Taylor, "*The Opening Arguments of the Phenomenology*," in Alasdair MacIntyre, *Hegel: A Collection of Critical Essays* (Notre Dame Press, 1976), pp. 151–187; Robert Pippin, *Hegel's Idealism: The Satisfactions of Self-Consciousness* (Cambridge

The logic of sense-certainty, then, is self-undermining. To have a purely immediate understanding of the world would be to have only pure experiences that could not be communicated or described in any way. To have a purely immediate understanding of the world is thus to have no understanding at all. Any actual understanding of the world, anything that we would count as knowledge, depends on linguistic abstractions that transcend the absolute singularity of sense-certainty. It is not possible to know the world in the purely immediate terms of classical empiricism, because to know the world is always to know it *under a description*. And to describe the world, to know it under a description, is to perceive it in some determinate way.

PERCEPTION

What we have shown so far is that if we are to know objects, we cannot eliminate everything that comes from ourselves as subjects. We cannot simply make ourselves passive receptacles, into which experience and thereby knowledge will flow. Rather, we have to make use of language, of abstract concepts, in order to describe the world in particular ways.

If we agree that all our concepts are human creations and nothing more, then Hegel's argument would already be complete: the activity of the subject makes any knowledge possible. But there seems no reason to grant anything of the sort. Even if knowledge is essentially linguistic or conceptual, there seems to be no reason to conclude that our language and our concepts cannot correspond to a world beyond ourselves. When we describe the world, we are not simply describing our own thoughts; rather we are describing objects and their qualities. This is the way I talk about the apple: it is red, it is round, and it is shiny. Granted, I cannot know the apple in the way sense-certainty suggests, experiencing it yet not describing it in any particular way. But my descriptions, even if always expressed in linguistic or conceptual terms, are descriptions not of myself but of the qualities of the objects that I observe, or perceive, in the world. We can reformulate a version of the theoretical standpoint, then, by saying that we are looking to describe the properties of the objects that we find in the world. This standpoint of perception, however, is already committed to a certain assumption about the world: that it is composed of things that exhibit a variety of properties. The properties, taken in one way, are distinct from one another. The apple's redness is not the same as its tartness;

University Press, 1989), pp. 116–125; Terry Pinkard, *Hegel's Phenomenology: The Sociality of Reason* (Cambridge University Press, 1994), pp. 20–28.

indeed, some tart apples are green, and some red apples are not tart at all. In this sense, the many properties of the apple are distinguished from the simple unity of the apple itself. At the same time, the properties are not really distinct, because they all are qualities of the apple that, in some sense, reflect its nature. If I say, "This red apple is tart," I am not reporting two wholly separate sensory experiences, namely redness and tartness. Rather I am saying that there is, in the world, a single object, this apple, that is somehow constituted to be both red and tart.

In these moments, taken together, the Thing as the truth of perception is completed, so far as it is necessary to develop it here. It is (a) an indifferent, passive universality, the *Also* of the many properties or rather "matters"; (b) negation, equally simply; or the *One*, which excludes opposite properties; and (c) the many *properties* themselves, the relation of the first two moments, or negation as it relates to the indifferent element, and therein expands into a host of differences; the point of singular individuality radiating forth into plurality. (115)

The question that now interests Hegel is what justifies our appeal to the relation described in (c). In the claim that the red apple is tart, what justifies our implicit claim that both the redness and the tartness emanate from the same basic nature of the apple? The standpoint of perception, if is it to be properly theoretical, cannot allow that this claim is any sort of assumption that we bring to bear on our perceptions of the world. Rather the claim must itself somehow be perceived in the world; we must somehow observe that the redness and the tartness are linked together in the unity of the apple.

There seem to be only two ways in which this possibly could happen. Either we observe the various properties and then infer that they are linked together, or we somehow directly observe the unity that links them together. The first alternative seems the most plausible, in the sense that we come to know apples by apprehending their properties. But not everything that we take to be a property of an object really is such a property. Not every quality that we perceive is in fact a quality of the object itself. When we mistakenly attribute a property to an object, we say that we are deceived: the object appeared to have a property that it turned out to lack. In such a case, we say that the perception, and thus the deception, was due not to the object but to ourselves. Because we were tempted to see the object in some particular way, we were blinded to its true qualities. Not every perception, then, is truly a description of the object. It might simply be a description of ourselves, of how we are tempted to view that object. To know the world, we must describe only the properties that objects truly have (116).

But what properties are those? What we call properties of objects may turn out to be perceptions and nothing more: not qualities of objects in themselves but merely descriptions of how objects appear to us. For instance, I perceive the apple as shiny. But if I take it into a dark room, it is no longer shiny. So is shininess really a property of the apple? In a real sense, the answer is no: rather the apple has a property such that it appears shiny, or simply opaque, under different conditions. The apple is physically constituted such that when the right sort of light is applied to it, the apple appears to us as shiny. But we can truly say that the reality of the object is not its shininess but the physical constitution that causes the appearance of shininess under the relevant conditions. The reality of the object is not the property of shininess but the lower-level properties that (under the right conditions) cause the apple to shine. In the language of modern philosophy, shininess is not a primary but a secondary quality: it is not in the object but in us. The true properties of the object, the primary qualities, are such that the apple appears to us as shiny under certain relevant conditions. For modern philosophers since Locke, the primary qualities are those invoked by modern (i.e., Gallilean/Newtonian) physics. On this view, properties like figure, extension, and number are primary qualities, while qualities like taste, sound, and smell are merely secondary qualities. The modern philosopher/physicist assumes that the latter sort of qualities are (a) merely perceptions in us; and (b) caused by, and entirely explicable in terms of, the primary qualities of ourselves and the external objects that affect us. On this view, the primary qualities, the properties invoked by modern physics, are the fundamental stuff of the physical world, the true nature of things. Notice how the standpoint of perception has shifted in this analysis. We began with the thought that what we perceive are the properties of objects, not simply facts about ourselves. But a perception now turns out to be a fact about what we experience, which is caused by the true properties of the object. Those true properties, the primary qualities of objects, are the only ones that are independent of our perception.

But how does the modern philosopher/physicist know what the truly primary qualities of objects are? In an important sense (though not, as we shall see, the only sense), our ideas of figure, extension, and number are no different from our ideas of tastes, sounds, and smells. For us, as Berkeley famously argued, all of these are merely perceptions: thoughts in ourselves that a certain object has a certain property. But any such thought, we have seen, can be wrong. Any perception we have might turn out not to be a property of an object but merely an event in our own minds, somehow produced in us by certain other, more fundamental qualities of an object.

To eliminate this possibility (to say nothing of more skeptical possibilities, e.g., that our perceptions are produced in us by a benevolent God or by an evil demon), we must show that what we take to be primary qualities really is the fundamental stuff of nature. We must eliminate the possibility that there might be a more fundamental physical theory, invoking an entirely different set of primary qualities, that could encompass and explain all our perceptions of figure and extension as mere effects of things as they are in themselves.

And this is what can never be done. To show that we had reached the fundamental structure of reality, we would have to move beyond any perception we might have of an object, anything we might be able to explain away, and examine the thing itself. This amounts to the second alternative described above: we somehow perceive the basic unity of the object directly, without the ordinary perception of determinate properties. (As we saw in Chapter 2, this is what would somehow have to be visible in Locke's special and ultimately imaginary microscope, the one that was good enough to tell us that we had reached the real essence of a thing.) But to perceive an object is always to perceive it in some determinate way. Without some relation to a perception that someone might have, a claim about a property of an object can never be verified in any way. Hence the notion of a thing, apart from any perception anyone might have of it, is an entirely empty and useless idea. This, of course, was Berkeley's argument against Locke's notion of physical substance, of "matter": the notion of a thing, apart from any properties we might detect through perception, is entirely meaningless.

Contrary to Berkeley, however, we do not have to conclude from this argument that there are no differences between primary and secondary qualities, that there are only secondary qualities, and thus that physical objects are nothing more than ideas in God's and our minds. We can agree with the modern philosopher/physicist that what he calls primary qualities really are more fundamental than secondary qualities, as long as we see the primacy of the primary qualities as derived from the explanatory power of physics, not from an account of reality itself. Since this primacy comes from our own scientific theories, there is a sense in which the unity of an object, what holds its various properties together, comes from ourselves as knowers:

At first, then, I become aware of the Thing as a *One*, and have to hold fast to it in this its true character; if, in the course of perceiving it, something turns up which contradicts it, this is to be recognized as a reflection of mine. Now, there also occur in the perception various properties which seem to be properties of the Thing, but the Thing is a One, and we are conscious that this diversity by which it would cease to be a One falls in us. So in point of fact, the Thing is white only to *our eyes*, *also* tart to *our* tongue, *also* cubical to *our* touch, and so one. We get the entire diversity of these aspects, not from the Thing, but from ourselves, and they fall asunder in this way for us, because the eye is quite distinct from the tongue, and so on. We are thus the *universal medium* in which such moments are kept apart and exist each on its own. Through the fact, then, that we regard the characteristic of being a universal medium as *our* reflection, we preserve the self-identity and the truth of the Thing, its being a One. (119)

As perceptions, our attributions of determinate properties to objects seem to refer only to secondary qualities, to events about us and not to the objects as they are in themselves. But if we see the holding together of the diversity of these perceptions as itself the work of our thinking (121–122), then the appeal to primary qualities (which constitute the essential unity of the object) is perfectly legitimate. The distinction between primary and secondary qualities is no longer a distinction between the reality of the object and the subjectivity of our perceptions, but rather a distinction that takes place within our thinking, between our explanations and the perceptions they explain. "The object is now for consciousness this whole movement which was shared between the object and consciousness" (123). What makes what we call primary qualities more fundamental is simply that we are able to use them to account for what we call secondary qualities.[2]

What have we learned in this argument? We began, in the wake of sense-certainty's self-undermining, with the thought that to know an object is to describe it in some particular way. When we describe an object, we describe it as a thing that has a particular property. But to count as knowledge, our description of any object has to be a true one: we must describe the properties that an object truly has. To confirm our descriptions of objects, we rely on our perceptions. But not every perception corresponds to a property of the object; some are more properly described as properties of ourselves. Thus, our talk of things and their properties necessarily falls into talk of primary and secondary qualities. Real knowledge of the physical world is knowledge of the primary qualities of objects. In speaking of primary qualities, we seem to be speaking of objects entirely as they are in themselves. But this is an illusion: the notion of a thing entirely distinct from our perceptions, entirely distinct from any property we might confirm that it has, is entirely idle. Our best descriptions of a thing, then, are not really descriptions of the thing as it is in itself. Rather they are simply better

---

[2] Further accounts of this discussion of perception can be found in Pippin, *Hegel's Idealism*, pp. 125–131; and Pinkard, *Hegel's Phenomenology*, pp. 28–34.

descriptions – in the sense that they manage to provide better explanations of the perceptions that we have. Just as sense-certainty's talk of pure experiences could not stand alone, since to know an object is to know it under a description, so also perception's talk of things and their properties cannot stand alone, since to describe a thing's true properties is just to explain it in a certain way. In studying the logic of sense-certainty, we learned that we cannot make sense of our talk of experiences, of sensations, unless we talk in the language of perception, of things and their properties. Now, in studying the logic of perception, we have learned that we cannot make sense of our talk of things and their (true) properties unless we talk in the language of scientific explanation, of theories and the observations that they explain.

THE INVERTED WORLD

We are now about to enter into the argument of what may be the densest and most confusing discussion of the entire *Phenomenology*, the section on "Force and the Understanding."[3] Hegel's discussions of force and the laws of forces involve some especially complicated reflections on the theoretical commitments of modern physics, and few readers of this book will have the scientific interest or competence to follow them. But there is a real question about whether Hegel himself had the scientific competence to make his discussions convincing to those who are well acquainted with physics. For our purposes, what matters most is what Hegel hopes to accomplish in this section of the book, and for that reason, it will be especially important to keep the bigger picture of his argument in view.

It is crucial to remember that Hegel is not trying to deny the possibility of a theoretical standpoint. He is not trying to deny the possibility of objective or scientific knowledge. Rather, he is trying to discredit a certain view of theoretical knowledge, one that is purged of any reference to human subjectivity. Instead of understanding Hegel as rejecting the notion of sense-experience, or the distinction between primary and secondary qualities, we should see him as identifying the presuppositions that make these understandings of the world possible, and productive of knowledge. If we are to gain knowledge of the world through our senses, Hegel is saying, we cannot simply experience the world; rather we must describe it

---

[3] My reconstruction of this especially difficult argument owes a great deal to Pippin, *Hegel's Idealism*, pp. 131–142. See also Pinkard, *Hegel's Phenomenology*, pp. 34–45; Hans-Georg Gadamer, "Hegel's 'Inverted World,'" in *Hegel's Dialectic: Five Hermeneutical Studies*, trans. Christopher Smith (Yale University Press, 1976), pp. 35–53; and Merold Westphal, *History and Truth in Hegel's Phenomenology* (Humanities Press, 1978), pp. 93–119.

conceptually, in terms of things and their properties. And if we are to have knowledge of how things really are as opposed to how things merely appear to us, we cannot simply compare our descriptions of the world to reality as it is in itself. Rather we must compare our descriptions of the world to one another, choosing those descriptions that have the most explanatory power.

But what does this explanatory power consist of? We have said that modern physics is able to vindicate its categories by explaining the secondary qualities in terms of the primary qualities. Now we have to know what makes such explanation successful. For not all possible explanations, all ways of accounting for a given phenomenon, are equally good. If we are not able to say what makes modern physical science (or anything else) successful as an explanation of the natural world, we will not be able to account for our understanding of physics as yielding genuine knowledge.

Hegel's own answer to this question will be: it is the practical context and the practical interests of human beings that allow them to choose between competing explanations, to identify particular theoretical candidates as successfully explaining our experience. This answer, of course, assumes the rejection of a purely theoretical standpoint. On Hegel's view, to explain the possibility of objective knowledge, we need to appeal to the nature of the human subject. And this is what the defender of the traditional theoretical standpoint will never allow. We have already seen that the defenders of this standpoint cannot account for their own claims to knowledge without invoking the conceptual apparatus of description and then of explanation. Now, to save the purely theoretical standpoint, the defenders of this view must tell us what makes a description a good explanation – without invoking any practical or subjective interests.

The traditional, purely theoretical candidate for this meta-explanation, this explanation of explanation, is generality. What makes a description an explanation, it might be said, is that it accounts for a set of phenomena in more general terms. On this view, we explain A and B in terms of C if we are able to see A and B as instances of C. The classical expression of this idea is provided by Plato's notion of a Form. What makes particular actions just, says Plato, is that they all share a common feature or property, a Form of Justice, which makes the actions what they are. On this view, the particular phenomena of the world are explained by a set of general features, the set of Forms, which constitute the fundamental structure of the world. As a scientific explanation, of course, Plato's account of Forms is notoriously weak. He is famously unclear about what Forms there are, and he spends relatively little time discussing specific Forms and the way they could explain particular phenomena. But as a philosophical claim about the nature of scientific explanation, Plato's account of Forms perfectly expresses the view of the pure theorist: that successful explanation consists not in satisfying any practical interests, but in providing a more general framework through which to comprehend the world.

In Hegel's discussion, this kind of general framework is described as a set of laws that governs the operation of forces in the physical world (148). There is some question about how Hegel is first able to introduce the notion of force into the argument (136), but the conclusion of the section on "Perception" was that the fundamental features of nature are those described in our best physical theories, and it seems reasonable for Hegel to assume that the physics of his day invoked force as an essential feature of its explanations. The notion of force, Hegel goes on to say, implies its action on something in the world, which Hegel then describes as a kind of soliciting force (137). Thus there are always (at least) two forces, each of which are independent; but since they clearly act on one another, there must be some way of describing how this interaction occurs. This, Hegel tells us, is the law of force. Even if some of Hegel's claims about force seem poorly motivated (are they justified by physical science, or by some sort of conceptual or philosophical necessity?), he seems on safe ground in holding that modern scientific theories are typically committed to a notion of scientific law. The question that Hegel then takes up (in 150 and following) is how laws provide deeper explanations of the phenomena they describe. A law, Hegel says, is supposed to provide necessity for a given event (151), but it seems to do this merely by making the event a single instance of the general regularity stated in the law (154). This is the sense in which laws are like Platonic forms: they comprehend the particular within the universal. They describe particular forces as instances of laws.

But how can generality provide any explanation? How would a Platonic form provide us with any real knowledge? A view like Plato's faces the following dilemma, itself suggested by Aristotle's famous criticisms. Either (1) the Form of Justice just is the property that particular just actions already have, or (2) it is some other sort of entity, different from the particular justice of particular actions yet somehow causally related to it. If (1) is right, then the appeal to the Form explains nothing. It merely states what we already knew: that these particular actions are just. (Hegel's own example [154] is a single occurrence of lightning.) To say that there is something called Justice that makes an action just does not say anything beyond calling it just. To provide a useful piece of knowledge, a theory must take us beyond our present understanding. And if we already understand that A and B are instances of the same phenomenon C, appealing to a general law or entity called C does not tell us anything new. We need to explain events in the world, not just to state and catalogue them.

This suggests that for the Platonic or "generalist" view to have any force, it must imply (2), the claim that a Form or general law is something distinct from the phenomena it is intended to explain. But then we must ask: how are we entitled to appeal to it? Suppose that the Form of Justice is something distinct from the justice of particular actions. In that case, we do not observe Justice; instead we regard Justice as the causal power which creates the particular justice that we do observe. But invoking the Form does not show us how this causal process works. To say that something called Justice makes particular actions just is not much different from saying that the gods or aliens make them just – unless we can observe and understand the causal process by which one of these entities does make the actions just. But the appeal to the Form does not provide this understanding; instead it seems to preempt this understanding through an appeal to an unobserved and unobservable power. In this sense, the appeal to the Form looks entirely dogmatic. We simply posit an entity, and a causal power, without explaining its relation to the particulars that we do observe. (If we posited another sort of Form to "explain" this relationship, as Aristotle pointed out, the whole process would begin again.)

The Platonic appeal to generality, then, does not help to clarify the nature of explanation. If a general rule or law is to be anything other than dogmatic, if it is to receive any sort of empirical confirmation, the rule or law cannot be an appeal to a new sort of causal power. Rather, the rule will have to be a statement of the regularities, properties, or patterns that we can and do observe. But we have not seen how such a statement can provide real knowledge, in the sense of explaining something that we did not already know.

But we do know that there are explanations that are both successful and powerful. So how can a scientific law be nothing more than an empirically observed regularity, yet still have genuine explanatory power? If Hegel's argument against Platonic views is right, the explanatory power cannot come from generality. Instead, Hegel suggests, the explanatory power must come from something like *novelty*. If a general rule or law is merely a way of describing the world, yet still has some privilege over other descriptions of the world, that privilege must come not from some formal feature like generality, but from the particular relationship between the particular descriptions in question. What gives an explanation its power is that it allows us to describe the world in a way that differs sharply from the descriptions that we had previously been tempted to offer.

In a dense and famously confusing discussion (157–160), Hegel packs this claim into a paradox that he calls "the inverted world." Traditional theoretical views like Plato's, Hegel reminds us, distinguish sharply between appearance and reality. We have seen that such views understand reality as something entirely distinct from appearance, yet somehow also causally related to it, such that the structure of the real (or "supersensible") world determines the structure of the apparent (or "sensible") world. But we have not been able to distinguish this sort of view from dogmatism, to say what it is that entitles the pure theorist to appeal to a real world entirely distinct from appearance. If we look closely at such views, Hegel suggests, we see that the warrant for this distinction comes not from the truth of the real or supersensible world – which we have no real access to – but rather from the nature of the apparent or sensible world, which is understood as defective in some way. Dissatisfied with the nature of the sensible world, the pure theorist inverts appearance into its opposite. For instance, because our world is characterized by change and decay, the Platonist invokes another world, characterized by eternal sameness. Views that distinguish sharply between appearance and reality, then, are driven not so much by an insight into the real but by a dissatisfaction with the apparent world, which the theorist is driven to invert into something entirely different.

This Hegelian account is meant to provide a practical explanation of the appearance–reality distinction, not a theoretical defense of it. For the pure theorist, Hegel's account of the inverted world is an embarrassment: what the pure theorist calls reality turns out to be, on closer inspection, merely the denial of appearance. The pure theorist's alleged insight into reality is thus unmasked, in the manner of materialist or secular explanations of religious belief, as a form of dissatisfaction with appearance. The purely theoretical standpoint cannot tolerate this unmasking, since the pure theorist demands precisely that we free ourselves from appearance and occupy ourselves only with reality. For Hegel, however, this unmasking is not an embarrassment; nor does it undermine either the appearance–reality distinction or the process of theoretical explanation. For Hegel, dissatisfaction with appearance is a perfectly respectable candidate for the source of explanatory power. What gives an explanation its force, Hegel is saying, is its ability to provide us with a new way of looking at the world, one that allows us to move beyond an old and dissatisfying view.

On this account, what drives the process of theoretical explanation is the practical context of human subjects. We find ourselves in situations in which our understandings of the world strike us as unsatisfying in particular ways. We are then driven to seek out new ways of looking at the world which enable us to resolve or avoid the practical problems that we bring to the theoretical context. What makes the new understandings of the world more powerful is not that they penetrate beyond appearance to a reality which is wholly distinct from appearance, but that they are able to take us beyond our present dissatisfactions. Or better: there is nothing wrong with our describing this movement as a movement from appearance to reality, as long as we understand that this movement does not take us outside the structure of human consciousness to something entirely beyond it. Rather, the entire process of theoretical explanation takes place within human consciousness, and is driven by the human subject's practical need to go beyond its present, and dissatisfying, understandings of the world.

FROM THEORY TO PRACTICE

What has just been said should itself seem unsatisfying. For we know nothing yet about what it means for us to find an understanding of the world dissatisfying, or to overcome this dissatisfaction in the right sort of way. At this point in his argument, Hegel can only appeal to these practical considerations in a vague and general way, for he has not yet provided an account of human practice, one that could show why his talk of practical interests is any more coherent than the traditional view of purely theoretical interests. All Hegel claims to have shown thus far is that the purely theoretical standpoint is unable to account for its own claims to knowledge.

Once again, this does not mean that there are no valid theoretical claims to knowledge, or that physical science lacks objectivity. Rather, Hegel's account assumes from the start that there is theoretical knowledge, and that we do recognize the claims of physical science as having objective force. The question is whether we can account for knowledge and objectivity without recognizing the practical dimension of human subjectivity. What Hegel takes himself to have shown is that anything that we would count as objective knowledge is not an unmediated insight into the nature of reality. Rather, a claim to theoretical knowledge is (1) a conceptual, linguistic statement of (2) the properties that a thing truly has that (3) we accept because it has explanatory power. Hegel takes himself to have identified these three features as what Kant would call transcendental conditions of knowledge, conditions that have to be met for anything to count as knowledge.

For Kant, however, the transcendental conditions of theoretical knowledge could be stated and defended in exhaustive fashion, as derived from the two forms of intuition and the table of twelve categories. For Hegel, however, no such exhaustive account of theoretical knowledge is possible, because any list of transcendental conditions misses the irreducibly *dynamic* character of theoretical knowledge. We have seen that Hegel derives his three transcendental conditions of knowledge in a serial manner: our talk of sense-experience, (1) as necessarily conceptual, devolves into talk of things and their properties; and then, (2) as necessarily directed to truth, into talk of appearance and reality; and then, finally, (3) as necessarily understood as explanatory, into a (as yet unfinished) practical account of explanatory power. In each case, the attempt to justify our claims to knowledge through contact with something outside our own thoughts comes to nothing, and we are left with a picture of human subjects comparing their thoughts, their various descriptions of the world, with one another. It is Hegel's claim that this sort of process could be productive of knowledge (or anything else) only if it were conceived in a dynamic fashion. Since theoretical activity is nothing more than the comparison of forms of consciousness, we need some way of accounting for the achievement of knowledge, the force of explanatory power, that captures its positive or productive character without a leap from consciousness to something outside of itself. So we have to account for theoretical knowledge as some sort of dynamic movement within consciousness, an interplay within our various descriptions of the world.

Thus it should be clear why no exhaustive list of transcendental conditions, no table of categories, is possible. Such an account cannot capture the dynamic character of explanation, a character that Hegel has already built into his own account of the conditions of theoretical knowledge. And even though we have not yet seen or understood Hegel's account of practical experience, it should be clear that the domain of the practical is perfectly suited to capture the dynamism that is the final result of Hegel's inquiry into theory. For no matter how it is conceived, our practical experience, our experience as agents, is an inherently dynamic process, a process through which we seek to transform both the world and ourselves. Hegel describes this process as "infinity" (160–161); as "the simple essence of life, the soul of the world" (162); and finally, as "absolute unrest of pure self-movement" (163). All of these descriptions are meant to capture the idea of an agent whose independence consists precisely in her power to act in and on the world, and thereby to transform herself. If the process of theoretical explanation has this dynamic character, it ought to be clear why a Hegelian account of explanation, a Hegelian account of theoretical knowledge, cannot terminate in a Kantian table of categories, but must press onward to an explicit and definite account of our practical experience.

CHAPTER 7

Practice

In Hegel's skeptical argument against the purely theoretical standpoint, we learned that a subject cannot attain anything that would count as knowledge by ridding itself of its subjective character, by simply attending to objects in their purest and most unmediated form. We saw that actual theoretical knowledge is impossible without the transcendental conditions that characterize any knowing self: its conceptual, descriptive nature, and then its practical interest in explanation. But it is important to see that we came to understand the nature of the knowing self in a serial or developmental manner. By examining the efforts of the theoretical self as it attempts to shake off its own, subjective character, we came to learn just what that character is, and why it is essential to theoretical knowledge. We came to understand the nature of the subject only through the subject's own efforts to deny that nature.

Now, as we have seen, Hegel's task is to describe the nature of the active or practical self, since on his account it is this practical self that is essential to the successful knowing of the theoretical self. To complete his account of explanation, and thus of theoretical knowledge, Hegel must describe the character of the practical interests that (on his view) allow us to understand certain theoretical descriptions of the world as carrying explanatory power. So it would seem to follow that Hegel's account would plunge next into various accounts of the practice of explanation, of the practical interests that it serves. But in fact he does nothing of the sort. Instead he switches his focus to a much more general account of the nature of agency. To the extent that the *Phenomenology* does offer an account of the practice of theoretical explanation, that account is delayed until the section on "Observing Reason" (Hegel's Chapter V, A).

There seem to be at least two important reasons for this shift. First, the sort of practical interest that theoretical explanation serves will be a particular kind of practical interest, and Hegel needs to be clear about what kind of practical interest that is. Second, and more crucially, since the practical interest Hegel has in mind is meant to play a crucial role in the rational justification of theoretical claims, he needs to explain what gives this practical interest its claim to rationality. Since, given Hegel's account of the theoretical self, there is no purely theoretical account of rational justification, claims to rationality must have their source in the essential character of practice, in the nature of agency. ("With self-consciousness, then, we have therefore entered the native realm of truth" [167].) It therefore makes sense for Hegel to enter first into a more general inquiry into the nature of action and practical rationality.

So what is it to be an agent, a practical self? Hegel begins by telling us that we already know the answer to this question, because we have seen that answer in the serial or developmental account of the theoretical self. What it is to be a practical subject, Hegel says, is just to be the sort of being that by rejecting what seems external to itself, learns that it has denied its own nature, and thereby comes to understand what it truly is. "But in point of fact self-consciousness is the reflection out of the being of sense and perception, and is essentially the return from otherness" (167).

At this point, this Hegelian claim should seem not just unproven but also so formal as to be without any real content. If we do not know the nature of the practical subject, how can it help to be told that a practical subject is one that rejects what is external to itself, and thereby denies its own nature? How can we understand this rejection and this denial unless we understand what the nature of the practical subject is?

But even this formal claim gives us some insight into Hegel's understanding of the practical realm. For the formal claim is a claim about opposition: the practical self is the sort of being that opposes itself to the world beyond itself. In emphasizing the thought of an agent opposed to everything outside itself, we reverse the developmental account of the theoretical self. In the theoretical case, we began with an attempt to eliminate the subject and focus only on the object; we then learned that subjectivity was essential to any account of the object. In the practical case, we will begin with an attempt to eliminate the object and focus only on the subject; we will then learn that a certain sort of objectivity is essential to being a subject. "Self-consciousness which is simply *for itself* and directly characterizes its object as a negative element . . . [will] learn through experience that the object is independent" (168). Hegel's claim about agency, then, should be understood like this: there are certain conditions, themselves external to an agent, that are required for agency itself. Just as there are subjective conditions of knowledge, so there are objective conditions, external constraints, that must hold if we are to understand and recognize ourselves as agents.[1]

To justify this claim, we deploy yet another skeptical or reductive argument, aimed this time at a non-Hegelian and thus allegedly impoverished conception of the practical self. Because we want to identify the objective or external conditions that are constitutive of human agency, we direct our skepticism against a conception of agency that assumes just the reverse: that an agent's projects are entirely self-contained, needing no reference to a world beyond the agent herself. In describing the incoherence of this wholly subjective conception of agency, we will come to understand the true nature of the practical self.

DESIRE

Imagine, then, a person whose agency was entirely self-contained. As an agent, such a person would have determinate goals, specific projects of action, but would be wholly unconcerned with the world beyond herself (". . . the sensuous world is for it an enduring existence which, however, is only *appearance*, or a difference which, *in itself*, is no difference" [167]). She would understand her ends and plans as deriving only from herself, as prompted by her own particular nature. Such an agent could only be motivated by her own desires: subjective, idiosyncratic promptings that direct her to act in a particular way. This view of human action, of course, is just the one held by the classical empiricists, by Hobbes and Hume, the view that has always dominated the Anglo-American philosophical tradition. On this view, to act is to be moved by a particular desire, and to act rationally is to do what is necessary or efficient to satisfy that desire.[2] There are things

---

[1] When I speak here of subjective conditions of knowledge and objective conditions of agency, it might seem like I am speaking of two very different sorts of things. But in fact I (and, I am saying, Hegel) mean to speak of the very same thing: norms. Norms of belief and of action are not fundamentally different; they each are standards that are meant to be authoritative for us. In that they are not properties of the objects of the physical universe, they are in one sense subjective, but since they are not subject to the arbitrary will of the individual, they are in another sense objective. How these norms get their authority is of course the deeper problem of this study, and I have already said that Hegel's answer will be that authoritative norms are ones that cohere with the subject's nature as a retrospective self-knower. This claim is still to be established in the argument; for now, Hegel is eliminating the possibilities that norms of belief could somehow come directly from the nature of the object (as in the theoretical standpoint criticized in the last chapter), or that norms of action could somehow come directly from the nature of the subject (the conception of agency to be criticized in this chapter).

[2] There is some question about whether Hobbes or Hume would have endorsed this view of rationality, although most Anglo-American interpreters have taken them to hold it. Taking an effective means to satisfy a desire is what Hobbes calls prudence, and he explicitly distinguishes it from reason.

that it is rational for us to do, but the account of their rationality must begin with a brute fact that cannot itself be given any rational justification: a subject's desire for an object. The goodness of an object is grounded simply in the fact of a subject's desire. When "self-consciousness is Desire in general," writes Hegel:

> Consciousness, as self-consciousness, henceforth has a double object: one is the immediate object, that of sense-certainty and perception, which however *for self-consciousness* has the character of a negative; and the second, viz. *itself*, which is the true *essence*, and is present in the first instance only as opposed to the first object. In this sphere, self-consciousness exhibits itself as the movement in which this antithesis is removed, and the identity of itself with itself becomes explicit for it. (167)

But the mere satisfaction of desire, Hegel goes on to say, is itself unsatisfactory. In desiring, we have seen, an agent is concerned only with herself as an agent; the world beyond the agent is without meaning. But to seek to satisfy a desire is itself to pursue an object beyond the self. "Desire and the self-certainty comes from superseding the other: in order that this supersession can take place, there must be this other. Thus self-consciousness, by its negative relation to the object, is unable to supersede it; it is really because of that relation that it produces the object again, and the desire as well" (175). Thus the desiring agent is constantly occupied with the seemingly irrelevant world of objects. To satisfy herself as an agent, the desiring self needs not another object but a confirmation of herself as an agent. ". . . [I]t is so only by superseding the object; and it must experience its satisfaction,

---

Reasoning for Hobbes is "the adding and subtracting of names," the deductively certain derivation of truths from the relations of our concepts. Prudential "reasoning," however, is never deductively certain: Hobbes says it is always a "presumption" or a "conjecture" that the chosen means will in fact satisfy our desire. He has in mind here a version of Hume's later argument about induction: our beliefs that a given object will satisfy our desire are based on our experience of the past, and we cannot assume that the inference to the future case will hold. When we turn out to be right, says Hobbes, "when the event answereth our expectations," we call it wisdom, but "in its nature it is but presumption" (*Leviathan*, Part I, chapter III).

Hume, for his part, seems to deny that anyone can be criticized as irrational if they choose not to take an effective or even a necessary means to a desired end; in such a case, we can just as fairly say that the agent did not desire the object all that much. The only failure of rationality that Hume seems to criticize in agents is their failure to recognize the connection between a means and an end, and this can better be seen as a failure of theoretical rather than practical rationality. In this sense Hume seems not to believe in practical rationality at all. See Elijah Milgram, "Was Hume a Humean?" *Hume Studies* 21 (1995), pp. 75–93, for a case to this effect.

All of this actually brings Hobbes and Hume closer to Hegel's argument, because Hegel's claim will be that there is something deeply anti-rational about a traditional empiricist or naturalist conception of action. That, I have just suggested, is something Hobbes and Hume themselves recognized, whereas most Anglo-American philosophers insist that a conception of practical rationality as merely instrumental is the most sensible account of practical rationality.

for it is the truth." And this satisfaction can be supplied only by another agent, by another person, who recognizes her as an agent and thus confirms her sense of herself:

On account of the independence of the object, therefore, it can achieve satisfaction only when the object itself effects the negation within itself; and it must carry out this negation within itself, for it is *in itself* the negative, and must be *for* the other what it *is*. Since the object is in its own self negation, and in being so is at the same time independent, it is consciousness. In the sphere of Life, which is the object of Desire, *negation* is present either *in an other*, viz. in Desire, or as a *determinateness* opposed to an indifferent form, or as the inorganic universal nature of Life. But this universal independent nature in which negation is present as absolute negation, is the genus as such, or the genus as *self-consciousness. Self-consciousness achieves its satisfaction only in another self-consciousness.* (175)

This famous passage introduces Hegel's notion of recognition, which on many accounts is Hegel's chief contribution to practical philosophy.[3] It is clear that Hegel himself would agree with some version of this claim, because he immediately declares that his argument has reached a crucial "turning-point." That agents require recognition by other agents is the first explicit appearance of Spirit in the argument, the first appearance of the idea of subjectivity that is the goal of the entire book:

A self-consciousness exists for a self-consciousness. Only so is it in fact self-consciousness; for only in this way does the unity of itself in its otherness become explicit for it. The "I" which is the object of its Notion is in fact not "object"; the object of desire, however, is only independent, for it is the universal indestructible substance, the fluid self-identical essence. A self-consciousness, in being an object, is just as much "I" as "object." With this, we already have before us the notion of *Spirit*. What still lies ahead for consciousness is the experience of what Spirit is – this absolute substance which is the unity of the different independent self-consciousnesses which, in their opposition, enjoy perfect freedom and independence: "I" that is "We" and "We" that is "I." It is in self-consciousness, in the Notion of Spirit, that consciousness first finds its turning-point, where it

[3] See for instance Jürgen Habermas, *Knowledge and Human Interests*, trans. J. Shapiro (Beacon Press, 1971); "Labor and Interaction: Remarks on Hegel's Jena *Philosophy of Mind*," in *Theory and Practice*, trans. John Viertel (Beacon Press, 1973), pp. 142–169; and Charles Taylor, *Multiculturalism and the Politics of Recognition* (Princeton University Press, 1992). The most famous attempt to make "the struggle for recognition" the central idea of the entire *Phenomenology* is the reading of Alexander Kojève, *Introduction to the Reading of Hegel*, trans. J. H. Nichols, Jr. (Basic Books, 1960). This Marxist interpretation was extremely influential for the reception of Hegel in the twentieth century: it was originally presented in a series of lectures that Kojève delivered in Paris in the 1930s, before an audience that turned out to include many if not most of the best-known French philosophers of the next few decades. For a more recent analytic account, see Paul Redding, *Hegel's Hermeneutics* (Cornell University Press, 1996), especially chapters 5 and 6.

leaves behind it the colorful show of the sensuous here-and-now and the nightlike void of the supersensible beyond, and steps out into the spiritual daylight of the present. (177)

So this is clearly an important moment in the argument. Still, it is not particularly clear what the argument is supposed to be. Many commentators are more than happy to appropriate the conclusion that human agents require recognition from others, especially in the service of communitarian critiques of liberal individualism – even if their enthusiasm for community goes far beyond anything that Hegel himself would have endorsed.[4] But most of these critiques get to their conclusions via their own critiques of liberal individualism, not by thinking through what Hegel actually means by an agent's need to "negate" the object, and then the need for the object to "effect the negation within itself." To justify and even to understand Hegel's emphasis on recognition, we need to make sense of these claims.

One way of reading the argument needs to be put immediately to the side. It is tempting to see Hegel as making a series of psychological claims, as providing an empirical description of what human beings need to be happy, to feel good about themselves. We might understand Hegel as pointing out that the desire for material things is obsessive and unfulfilling: as soon as one has a desired object, there is a desire for more and better objects, until one is consumed by the quest for objects and no longer able to enjoy oneself. We might then understand Hegel as praising the respect and admiration of others as a deeper and more lasting good, one that any person requires and continues to enjoy no matter how much she owns. We might understand Hegel as claiming that the psychological nature of human beings is such that without recognition by other human beings, without a sense that one is valued by others, no real happiness is possible.

These empirical or psychological claims seem entirely plausible, and in some form they are almost certainly true. But they have nothing to do with Hegel's argument, for they lack the necessity appropriate to philosophical claims. Hegel is not trying to give an empirical, psychological description of human agency; rather he is trying to say, in philosophical or purely rational terms, what it is to be an agent. The claims about the insufficiency of mere desire and the need for recognition, then, must be understood as necessary conditions for understanding oneself as an agent. When Hegel says that a desiring agent does not really want the object but rather to confirm her sense of herself, he cannot mean that physical enjoyment is less satisfying

---

[4] See for instance Taylor, *Multiculturalism and the Politics of Recognition*.

than a feeling of self-esteem. Instead he must mean something like this: that desire-based action is incoherent without an understanding of oneself as a rational agent, an understanding that itself implies a reference to other rational agents as sources of recognition.

We can understand this claim if we recognize that for a human agent, to pursue a desire is not just to be pulled by a physical force. Rather, it is to make an intentional, at least potentially conscious judgment that the desire is worth satisfying, and thus that the desired object is worth having. And to say that an object is worth having is not just to report on one's own idiosyncratic state. Rather, it is to make a judgment that carries a claim to objectivity, and that is automatically open to rational assessment. To say that a thing is worth having is not just to say that I want it, but also to say that any similarly situated agent has good reason to pursue a similar object. This is already a normative claim, a claim that others would and should agree with my judgment about the value of the object. In staking this claim to normativity, the desiring agent implicitly invokes a reference to a community of others, a set of rational beings that would assent to the agent's judgment of value. It is the (presumed) agreement of these others that constitutes the demand for recognition. To demand to be recognized is not to ask for the good wishes of others, but to expect their agreement to one's own claims about what it is rational to do. And since every decision to satisfy a desire implies a claim about what is rational to do, every desire-based action implies the demand for recognition. The expected agreement of rational beings is thus a necessary condition of agency, itself not based on any desire, yet built into every project of action.[5]

---

[5] See also the account offered by Robert Pippin, *Hegel's Idealism: The Satisfactions of Self-Consciousness* (Cambridge University Press, 1989), pp. 157–158; and Terry Pinkard, *Hegel's Phenomenology: The Sociality of Reason* (Cambridge University Press, 1994), pp. 49–53. The account offered here is closer to Pippin's than to Pinkard's.

The argument raises the more general issue of the relationship between desire-based or even egoistic conceptions of practical rationality to ethical or universalizability requirements. A well-known attempt to make the relationship extremely tight is Alan Gewirth's *Reason and Morality* (University of Chicago Press, 1980). As I understand Hegel's argument, he would reject Gewirth's claim that one's understanding of oneself as a rational agent implies a commitment to ethical or universalizability requirements. The connection between rationality and recognition requires only that desiring agents affirm a commitment to norms that they understand as applying to all rational agents; there is no further requirement that those norms recognize the value and/or the interests of all rational agents in some sort of equal fashion. To put the point another way: if agents claim that they have good reason to pursue some desired objects, they are also committed to the claim that other similarly situated agents also have good reasons for pursuing those objects, but they are not yet committed to saying that they have reasons for thinking that those other agents *should* have those objects. That further claim requires additional premises of some sort, which Hegel introduces only in the subsequent discussion of master and slave. As I understand it, this argument concerns the task of *justifying* norms to all other rational agents, and this interest in justification is what is required

Now let's put this way of understanding the argument back into Hegel's own language. The desiring agent is saying that what is crucial is not the object but the agent's own negation of the object. In the language I have used, this means that an agent pursuing a desired object is saying not that an object is good in itself, but that the object is good for the agent to have. But to say that an object is good for the agent to have is to make a rational judgment that the object is worth pursuing. Without this judgment, having the object is meaningless, which is another way of saying that what ultimately drives the project of action is not the object, nor even the negation of the object (the agent's having of it), but a subject's own negation of itself (the agent's judgment that she should subordinate her own agency to the pursuit of this particular object). What ultimately drives the project of action is the claim that some particular action is rational, and this kind of claim is ultimately not a claim about just this particular agent. Rather, it is a claim about *what rational agents ought to do*. The claim thus implies a reference to a community of rational agents who are presumed to share this judgment, since they too are rational agents.

What the claim does not imply – despite what any communitarian reading of Hegel would like to say – is the reference to any actual community of agents who explicitly endorse the particular agent's judgment that the object is worth pursuing. Hegel is not saying that one cannot rationally pursue an object unless other people give clear confirmation that the project of action is a good one. That claim may be empirically and psychologically plausible: it is extraordinarily difficult to pursue your own vision of what is good when those around you regard it as foolish or even wicked. But it is not in any sense rationally incoherent. What is incoherent, however, is to pursue your own vision of what is good without making normative claims about what is good for you and other (similarly situated) rational agents to do. The recognition that Hegel is talking about here is not the actual confirmation of actual others; it is instead the idealized but always presumed agreement of the community of rational agents. A rational agent who endorses any project of action is always already making a normative claim, and the agent's commitment to the norm implies a commitment to membership in a kind of community of rational agents, all of whom affirm the norm as their own. It is this idealized community – an "I" that is "We" and a "We" that is "I" – that is our first glimpse of what Hegel means by Spirit.

---

to make the connection between agent-centered rationality and ethical or universalizable norms (see note 7). The interest in justification cannot itself be justified on merely egoistic grounds, which is exactly why Gewirth's argument is doomed to failure.

MASTER AND SLAVE

Now we need to know: what is it to be a rational being? What does it mean to regard oneself as part of a community of at least potentially rational beings? What sort of constraints, if any, does this understanding of ourselves place on the practice of our agency? What can we say, if anything, about what a rational being values?

It is at this point that Hegel launches into what is perhaps his most famous discussion, that of lordship and bondship (178–196). He tells us that in order to realize their senses of themselves as agents, human beings must risk their lives in violent conflict with each other. "They must engage in this struggle, for they must raise their certainty of being *for themselves* to truth, but in the case of the other and in their own case. And it is only through staking one's life that freedom is won" (187). These conflicts end either in death – a meaningless non-satisfaction ("the *natural* negation of consciousness, negation without independence, which thus remains without the required significance of recognition" [188] – or in the enslavement of one of the combatants. "[T]hey exist as two opposed shapes of consciousness; one is the independent consciousness whose essential nature is to be for itself, the other is the dependent consciousness whose essential nature is simply to live or to be for another. The former is lord, the other is bondsman" (189). This last outcome would seem to be satisfying for the master or lord, who is able to satisfy his desires through another person who recognizes him as superior (190). But this satisfaction turns out to be illusory. The superior master turns out to need the humble slave for his own sense of self (191–193), while the slave, seemingly condemned to a life of meaningless labor (194), comes to recognize the true value of agency in work, through which human beings can transform the objects of the natural world into their own creations, the tangible and lasting expressions of their own agency (195). Of course, the slave is not able to control the products of his labor, but for Hegel, this fact itself serves to highlight the point that what matters in the activity of work is not the profit to be made from one's labor, nor the specific product of that labor, but rather the fact that the product of one's labor is the expression of the laborer's own agency. From this Hegel concludes that the true nature of rational agency, the real source of value, is expressed in the slave's consciousness of his own freedom (197).

As with Hegel's treatment of desire, we are tempted to regard this argument as a series of empirical or psychological claims. It might seem that Hegel is saying that what human agents really enjoy above all else is their freedom, and that they can come to realize this if they go through the sort of experience described in the narrative of master and slave. Viewed this way, Hegel's argument looks like a psychological comparison between various kinds of lives, to be confirmed by our actually living those lives – or at least by our examining those lives as lived by others.

In this case, however, the psychological claims seem more dubious, even obnoxious, than plausible. It seems absurd to say that the life of a slave is more satisfying than that of a master; nor does it seem right to say that human beings appreciate their agency and their freedom only when they have risked their lives and lived as slaves. (That last claim would justify some rather frightening educational practices, all in the name of human freedom.) Here we have even more reason to reject an empirical or psychological understanding of the argument, and to seek out an argument from the nature of rational agency itself. Clearly Hegel's conclusion is saying something like this: that any rational agent necessarily regards herself and all other rational agents as free, and values this freedom above all else. The question is how to understand this claim, and how to connect it to the narrative of master and slave.

We can begin, once again, by considering the negation of Hegel's claim: that a rational agent might value something other than freedom as the supreme good. That is, we must consider the possibility that a rational agent is concerned not so much with the ability to choose, but rather with certain objects of choice, with some good external to her willing. Call this other, external good "G." If Hegel's claim about freedom is false, then we can say that a rational agent has good reason to pursue G above anything else.

Given the previous argument about recognition, we can also say that a rational agent should regard every other agent as having a good reason to pursue G above everything else. But if that is so, then we are left with a constant potential for conflict: everyone always has good reason for doing anything in their power to obtain G. The result is just the state of war described by Hobbes: a world in which there is always the potential for violence and death, since everyone always has a good reason to do whatever she understands as necessary to obtain G.[6]

---

[6] Hobbes himself says that all human beings value security, the protection from death and violence. And he also says that they should, and do, value security over freedom. So if we regard our highest good G as security, is this already not the negation of Hegel's argument? Not necessarily: it is important to understand that Hobbes is not saying that human beings do not have good reasons to kill others in pursuit of security. In fact he says we often do have such reasons, if we cannot assure ourselves that those others will not hurt us first. Our inability to assure ourselves of that is the main cause of the state of war; that we all value security is exactly why we end up in violent conflict with one another.

This Hobbesian outcome is a philosophical conclusion, not an empirical prediction. In this hypothetical argument, we know nothing about the actual nature of our imagined supreme good G. It may well be that G is so plentiful or so easily available that there is little or no potential for actual conflict. But this is beside Hegel's point. He is not arguing that if G were the supreme good, human beings would in fact be likely to engage in radically destructive conflict. Rather, Hegel is making a claim about what is ideally rational: on the view that we are entertaining, a world in which there is the constant potential for life-or-death struggle is what we can call the most rational outcome, the state of affairs that would obtain if every person did what they have most reason to do. The important point is the theoretical or philosophical one: if G were the supreme good, everyone would have good reason to resort to violence, to endanger the lives of others, if this were necessary to obtain G.

But this last view, Hegel claims, is absurd. No rational agent in fact believes that the best or most rational state of affairs would be one in which anyone would be justified in using violence against anyone else. Every rational agent needs to be alive to enjoy G, no matter what G turns out to be. So if it is false that the Hobbesian state of war might be the most rational state of affairs, and if we still regard G as the supreme good, then we must say that in cases of potential conflict over G, the most rational state of affairs is one in which some rational agents are allowed to have G, and others are simply deprived of it. Since every rational agent has good reason to want G, we have no rational way of discriminating between those who are allowed to have G and those who are not. From the point of view of rational justification, this division between the haves and the have-nots is entirely arbitrary; it can be based on nothing more than force. And this is just a world in which some are masters and some are slaves. If we agree with Hegel (and Hobbes) that being alive is always necessary for enjoying G, then we must say that in cases of potential conflict over G, the most rational state of affairs is one in which some persons are arbitrarily subject to the rule of others.

But this, for reasons we have already suggested, is also absurd. On this way of thinking, the most rational state of affairs is one that includes an essential reference to non-rationality, to the arbitrary rule of one person by another. Slavery is just that condition in which power is detached from reason-giving: slaves must obey not because they have been given good reason to obey, but merely because they have been commanded to obey. Whether actual obedience is secured by violence or threat of violence, or by the thought (accepted by all too many masters and slaves alike) that the enslaved are less than fully rational, the point remains in force. Slavery is in every case a practice in which the enslaved are not given a rational justification for their enslavement. Either justification is replaced with force, or justification amounts to the self-undermining claim that the enslaved are not competent to receive justification in the first place. In either case, the reason for slavery is lost.

This argument may seem too strong. It may look as if Hegel is arguing that violence and slave-holding are so irrational and self-contradictory that these coercive practices make no sense. But of course we know exactly why they make sense to a great many people, and we know that the practices have continued to flourish in a depressingly familiar way. Hegel is not saying that violence and slave-holding are irrational in the sense that they are self-undermining for the agent who engages in them, that the practices will simply collapse under the weight of their own incoherence. Hegel is not saying, appearances to the contrary, that coercive agents cannot have what they "really" want.

What he is saying is rather that violence and slave-holding are inconsistent with agents' understandings of themselves as rational beings. Of course, this kind of understanding is all too easily bracketed for selfish gain, but if one attends closely to it, Hegel claims, one will understand the practical incoherence of coercive practices. We have seen that understanding oneself as a rational being implies understanding the objects that one decides to pursue as rationally worth pursuing, and we have seen that this claim implies the expected agreement of the whole community of rational beings. What I recognize as worthy is what I take all others to recognize as worthy as well. So if I decide to pursue some good G, I must allow that every other person has just as good reason to pursue G. And that means that in cases of potential conflict over G, there is no rational way to justify my having G, and others' being unable to have it. And so my claim that G is worth having always contains the threat of irrationality: in showing why I have reason to pursue G, I constantly threaten to reject, in an entirely arbitrary fashion, others' reasons to have it.[7]

---

[7] I do not take this argument of Hegel's to be saying that any rational agent is rationally required to refrain from violence or slave-holding (see the discussion in note 5). The practical incoherence here comes in the public articulation of any norms that would claim to "justify" violence or slave-holding. Violent or slave-holding agents are committed to norms that other agents are supposed to accept, and yet those norms cannot be articulated to them as justifications for their victimhood. The violence or slave-holding can be given a (purely egoistic) justification, but the victimization cannot be given any justification at all; it is simply a non-rational effect of the conduct that is taken to be rational. As to why this effect should be rationally acceptable, there is no answer at all. It is in the attempt to justify norms to all others that this sort of non-rational effect must be accounted for. But since norms

Recall that this argument began with the assumption that some external good G was worth having above all else. If this claim cannot be rationally justified without an essential reference to irrationality, then we must consider rejecting the assumption. That is, we must consider the possibility that no external good, no object of choice, could be rationally superior to the faculty of choice itself, to the freedom of the will. Instead of holding that freedom is valuable insofar as it allows us to secure good objects, we must turn to the opposing, Kantian view: that freedom is itself the supreme good, and that all other things are good only insofar as they are chosen by free or rational wills. Only this view, Hegel claims, can avoid practical incoherence; only this view can rationally evaluate cases of potential conflict over goods without reference to arbitrary force.

It is from this inverted perspective that we can understand Hegel's claim that only the slave, not the master, is in a position to appreciate the value of freedom. This claim does not imply the now even more ghoulish thought that *Arbeit macht frei*, that only toil and suffering can reveal the true meaning of freedom. The opposing positions of master and slave do not illustrate the psychology of human freedom; rather they represent opposing conceptual positions about the nature of the good and its relation to the will. The master is in the position of defending his overriding pursuit of external goods, and he can do this only by rationally justifying his status as a master over the slave. To confirm this justification, the master needs the assent of the slave, which the master's own justification for slavery has already affirmed as in no sense meaningful. The master is thus in the practically incoherent posture of justifying his rejection of justification. The slave, on the other hand, is perfectly suited to illustrate the overriding value of the free will. The slave is stripped of every external good, all his activities devoted to serving the wants of the master. Even if the slave were to value some object, he could not pursue it without the consent of his master. Without freedom, the slave's claims to value are without meaning. The slave works, but the results of that work are not his; to understand them as his own, to understand his product as a thing worth working for, the slave must be in the position of choosing that work for himself. And this perfectly illustrates Hegel's own claim: that freedom is the supreme good,

typically serve as public standards of justification (a point most famously emphasized in Habermas' communicative ethics), violent or slave-holding agents are in the position of being committed to norms that they cannot publicly articulate. This is not rationally incoherent (nor, despite what some of Habermas' stronger arguments have suggested, inconsistent with being a linguistically competent speaker) but rather a practical incoherence that would arise if the agents ever tried to explain the standards they claim that all rational agents ought to endorse to those agents themselves.

and indeed the necessary condition of our rationally affirming anything else as good.[8]

FREEDOM WITHOUT CONTENT

So far we have seen that to be a subject is to regard oneself as one of a potential community of rational agents, and to value freedom as necessary for any such agent. But what does it mean to value freedom? Does the value of freedom really place any constraint on the subject, as Hegel wants to suggest? It would seem instead that freedom represents the absence of constraint: the ability to choose as one sees fit.

Still, a free agent must choose something, and choose it on the basis of reasons. As we have already seen in our discussion of desire, merely to want something is not yet to have a reason for choosing it. One chooses something because one understands it as worth having, not because one feels somehow compelled to choose it. But we have also seen in our discussion of lordship and bondage that no object of choice is more valuable than the faculty of choice itself. That someone has chosen an object is a necessary condition for its having value.

We seem trapped in a kind of dilemma. Freedom without content is vacuous: we must explain what a free will would choose, and why the free will would choose in that way. But if we supply the content for the choice from outside the nature of the free will, we are placing a kind of constraint on the will that is inconsistent with its freedom. Freedom with external content is arbitrary: it demands that the will submit to something beyond itself. The free will must be given some reason to will in some particular way, but the particularity of every object of choice seems to threaten the absolute freedom of the will.

The only way out seems to be the *formalist* one: what the free will chooses is somehow freedom itself. That is, what the free will chooses is to exercise its freedom. But how? Simply by proclaiming its absolute independence from the rest of the world? This is the sort of view that Hegel associates with Stoicism: the assertion that a free and rational agent is utterly superior to, and utterly untroubled by, the natural and even the social world. But what sort of life will the Stoic lead? There seems to be no particular way to answer this question, except to assert the value of freedom and rationality itself: "Stoicism, therefore, was perplexed when it was asked for what was called

---

[8] For some further accounts of this stretch of argument, see Pippin, *Hegel's Idealism*, pp. 156–163; and Pinkard, *Hegel's Phenomenology*, pp. 53–63.

a 'criterion of truth as such,' i.e. strictly speaking, for a *content* of thought itself. To the question, *What* is good and true, it again gave for answer the *contentless* thought: The True and the Good shall consist in reasonableness. But this self-identity of thought is again only the pure form in which nothing is determined. The True and the Good, wisdom and virtue, the general terms beyond which Stoicism cannot get, are therefore in a general way no doubt uplifting, but since they cannot produce any expansion of the content, they soon become tedious" (200).

To relieve this tedium, to exercise the will that the Stoic can only proclaim as free, we need some particular content, some specific project of action. But any such project, we have already seen, can only bind the subject to an arbitrary goal. The free will must lash out against such restriction as inconsistent with its freedom. Perhaps, then, the free will can exercise its freedom by lashing out in just this way: by rejecting any particular project that might suggest itself as plausible. This is the position that Hegel associates with ancient skepticism: "the realization of that of which Stoicism was only the Notion" (201). The Stoic wanted to proclaim his absolute freedom, but he could find no outlet for its supposedly free agency. The skeptic finds that outlet by rejecting the standards and values he finds in his everyday life. None of these standards and values, he claims to prove through his techniques of skeptical argument, do we *know* to be valid beyond any doubt. Given any criterion of truth or rightness, we can always ask: but how do we really know? The skeptic proves his freedom by taking the standards and values of his particular community, the dictates of appearance and custom, and showing them to be nothing more than that. None of these standards and values is compelled by reason, and the skeptic is under no obligation to follow them. By demonstrating this point again and again, by continually refuting the rational claims of his local standards and values, the skeptic proclaims his absolute freedom and independence from reality. His goal is the same tranquility that the Stoic hoped to achieve, but since the skeptic achieves this goal through the exercise, not simply the consciousness, of his freedom, his position represents a kind of advance.

But not a sufficient advance. Since the skeptic's activity is precisely the refutation of customary standards and values, that activity is essentially dependent on those standards and values that it takes to have no reality. On the one hand, the skeptic, like the Stoic, wants to assert his absolute independence. But to assert this, the skeptic must turn against something in particular, and in doing so, he refutes his and the Stoic's own claim to be free of particular standards and values. But while the Stoic was merely puzzled by this impasse, unable to concern himself with the particular, the skeptic plunges into the impasse in an eager yet ultimately confused way. The skeptic freely admits the particularity and thus the meaninglessness of his customary standards and values: his very point is to point out this particularity and meaninglessness. But the skeptic also admits that his concern with the particular is essential to his own independence. The skeptic is thus in the position of asserting that the particular is both essential and unessential. For Hegel, ancient skepticism is *defined* by its inability and indeed its unwillingness to face this contradiction: "It does not bring these two thoughts of itself together. At one time it recognizes that its freedom lies in rising above all the confusion and contingency of existence, and at another time equally admits to a relapse into occupying itself with what is unessential . . . Point out likeness or identity to it, and it will point out unlikeness or non-identity; and when it is now confronted with what it has just asserted, it turns round and points out likeness or identity. Its talk is in fact like the squabbling of self-willed children, one of whom says A if the other says B, and in turn says B if the other says A, and who by contradicting *themselves* buy for themselves the pleasure of continually contradicting *one another*" (206).

The reference to childhood is absolutely crucial here. For what characterizes the skeptic's position, what constitutes its refusal to face its own contradictions, is not any sort of failure of knowledge, an inability to grasp the truth. Rather, the skeptic's failure is a kind of ability to face the truth that it knows all too well. And what it takes to face this truth, Hegel thinks, is not some sort of intellectual achievement, some moment of insight into a deeper truth, but rather a kind of maturity.

Recall that we are faced with a problem of reconciliation. On the one hand, Hegel takes himself to have shown that the central feature of our agency is our sense of ourselves as free. The value of freedom, he has argued, transcends any sort of value that might be given to particular objects of choice. Thus the free agent is always able to reject any particular object of choice as inconsistent with her freedom. But on the other hand, the free agent is one who does choose, and must choose, particular objects at particular times. The problem is thus to reconcile the infinite freedom of the agent with the inevitable particularity of any object of choice.

But this reconciliation does not happen through any sort of intellectual insight. Both the infinite freedom of the agent and the inevitable particularity of the objects of choice are, for Hegel, deep and unshakable truths. What constitutes the failure of Stoicism and skepticism is not a failure to recognize these truths, but a childish desire to run away from them. The Stoic simply tries to deny our entanglement in the particularity of the world. The skeptic admits this entanglement in one sense but denies it in another. By constantly refuting the truth of appearance and custom, the skeptic both affirms and denies that appearance and custom are essential to the free and rational agent. Skepticism is more sophisticated than Stoicism, but it achieves this sophistication only through a kind of deeper self-deception: it denies its own denial of particularity. Once this denial is faced, we are left with only the bitter realization of the truth of our predicament: our ability to transcend any specific particularity, and our simultaneous inability to achieve something utterly beyond particularity.

This bitter realization is what Hegel calls the Unhappy Consciousness. It is characterized by both a desire to leave the finite world and a realization that we cannot do so. As free and rational agents, we are not bound to any particular form of life, but if our free and rational agency is to have any meaning or content, we must choose some particular form of life. This is Hegel's philosophical reconstruction of Christian spiritual longing: we are pure souls who cannot ourselves transcend the impurity of this physical existence. In more traditional Christian theology, this contradiction is resolved externally, through the mediation of a savior. The appearance of Christ on earth – the infinite reality of God displayed in finite, human form – symbolizes for the believer the possibility of her own salvation. Hegel, in contrast, retains the symbolism of the Christ figure but seeks to understand the reconciliation of the infinite and the finite in a way that rationally articulates the theologically inexplicable moment of grace. He does this by understanding Christian spiritual longing, the despairing perspective of the Unhappy Consciousness, not as an insight into the truth of the human condition, but (like Stoicism and skepticism before it) as a particular, and particularly immature, attitude toward that truth. The Stoic and the skeptic attempted to flee from particularity; the Unhappy Consciousness admits that this cannot be done, and is thus plunged into despair. But this despair is equally a desire to flee the world; once we accept that this cannot be done, once we finally face the reality of our particularity, we can look back on our previous attempts to flee as foolish and futile. By seeing these forms of thought as successive attempts to avoid what cannot be avoided, by bringing them under a narrative that takes us from immature frustration to a mature acceptance of what cannot be changed, we turn the despairing attitude of the Unhappy Consciousness on its head – without an external form of salvation. Seen from the biographical perspective of the maturing individual, the inevitable particularity of our agency becomes not an occasion for despair, but the only realm in which we might be capable of exercising our free and rational agency. The infinite freedom of the agent is in fact at odds with the particularity of any object of choice. But whether we see this as an occasion for despair depends entirely on the perspective from which we understand these truths. For the Unhappy Consciousness, the understanding of the truths is an occasion for despair and for spiritual longing. From Hegel's biographical perspective, however, the despairing attitude of the Unhappy Consciousness is itself an immature longing to flee the world. For the mature individual, the world is not a place that can or should be fled.[9]

FROM AGENCY TO CULTURE

We began this chapter in an attempt to characterize the nature of the practical self, to explain the distinctive features of our agency. We began, skeptically, with the thought that there were no such features: that agents were bound by no external constraints, that they simply pursued their own individual desires, their own entirely idiosyncratic projects of action. But we learned that this thin perspective was insufficient: to be an agent is to be governed by a sense of oneself as both rational and free, and to value this sense of oneself above all external goods.

The problem then becomes how to understand the force of this supposedly thicker understanding of agency. What does it mean to understand ourselves as rational and free? What must a free and rational agent do? Once again we turned to a skeptical thought: there is nothing that such an agent must do, because to be free means not to be bound to any particular form of life.

Hegel does not deny this thought. Rather he shows us – through the historical examples of Stoicism, skepticism, and Christian spiritual longing (the Unhappy Consciousness) – how our sense of ourselves as infinitely free brings us hard up against another undeniable feature of our agency, namely that we must exercise our freedom on particular objects of choice. The turn to historical narrative is hardly accidental here.[10] First, since Hegel's

---

[9] See also Pinkard's account of these sections: *Hegel's Phenomenology*, pp. 63–78.
[10] It might fairly be objected here that the entirety of Hegel's argument in the *Phenomenology* is historical. For instance, it seems clear that Hegel's argument in the chapter on "Consciousness" (discussed in chapter 6 of this book) is his critique of the theoretical project of early modern philosophy (discussed in this book's chapter 2), concentrating especially on its empiricist strand. And it seems clear that the arguments we have just discussed here – the discussions of desire and of master and slave – are Hegel's accounts of the issues discussed in this book's chapter 3, the issues that occupy classical modern political philosophy from Hobbes through Rousseau. Still, Hegel does not make those historical connections as explicit as he does from this point on in the argument, and there seem to be important reasons for that. The theoretical projects and then the practical projects

point is precisely to show that we as agents are inevitably entangled in the particular circumstances of life, he illustrates the point through examples drawn from our own history and culture. Second, since Hegel wants not just to convince us of the inevitable particularity of our agency, but also to convince us not to see this particularity as in fatal conflict with our infinite freedom, he needs to show us actual examples of individuals who *did* see these features of our agency as locked in fatal conflict. By looking back at the history of their failed attempts to avoid the truth of our agency, we can come, retrospectively, to see the desire to flee from the particularity of our circumstances as futile and foolish. It is only from the perspective of retrospective narrative that we can understand this desire as immature.

In this sense the history of Western culture, then, becomes the proper and indeed the central object of Hegel's philosophical attention. In our account of the theoretical self, we saw that we could not describe the conditions of knowledge without taking into account our nature as agents. Now, in our account of the practical self, we have learned that we cannot understand our nature as agents, as free and rational beings, without turning to the specific historical circumstances that shape our choices and projects. The attempt to characterize our free and rational agency from an independent, ahistorical perspective is doomed to failure; there is simply no particular form of life that a free agent must choose. But a historical inquiry will not just be a detailing of the specific historical circumstances that have shaped the exercise of our free agency. History is not just the repository of forms of cultural life, choices, and events thrown into a kind of warehouse of the past. Rather, history is the past organized into a meaningful narrative, the forms of cultural life organized in a way that tells us something about ourselves. What sort of meaning could this narrative convey? Hegel's hope is that the narrative of history will provide us with a kind of reconciliation to the particularity of our agency. To see this particularity as not in fatal

---

of early modern philosophy are chosen not for their historical importance, but rather because they represent certain philosophically extreme and thus instructive positions: an account of knowledge as purely passive or receptive, and an account of agency as purely active or self-contained. When these arguments fail, Hegel wants to diagnose this failure by understanding the project of classical modern philosophy as a part of a larger historical narrative that begins with much earlier developments, including ancient Greek philosophy and the birth of Christianity. If Hegel were to discuss the history of modern philosophy in explicit terms at the start of the book, he would be obscuring his essentially connected claims that (1) modern philosophy represents an especially pure form of philosophical aspiration; and (2) modern philosophy takes on this pure aspiration because of its relation to a larger cultural story, one that includes pre-modern cultural developments that modern philosophy itself was inclined to ignore. So we cannot understand the true historical importance of modern philosophy until we turn to this larger history – which, in turn, we will not see the reason for until we have discredited the pure (and thus ahistorical) aspirations of modern philosophy itself.

conflict with our infinite freedom, to see our agency as not threatened by our entanglement in culture and history, we need to see that culture and that history as teaching us that we have overcome our earlier, futile efforts to insist on an unrestrained conception of freedom. To reconcile freedom with culture requires a kind of maturity, and only a historical narrative can show us that we have achieved it.

CHAPTER 8

Culture

To this point our presentation, though highly compressed, has managed to track the main arguments of the first two chapters of the *Phenomenology*, "Consciousness" and "Self-Consciousness." As we approach the later, mainly historical chapters of the book, however, the length and complexity of Hegel's discussions, together with the limited aims and length of this book, make even a compressed summary impossible. Since we will not be able to follow the specifics of all of Hegel's historical discussions, I am going to adopt a two-part approach to the remainder of the text in this long chapter. On the one hand, my focus will be on the general issue of what Hegel's turn to history is meant to accomplish. In what sense is his developmental account of Western culture intended to advance the philosophical argument of the first two chapters of the *Phenomenology*? On the other hand, my answer to that question will include a kind of sketch of the developmental account itself, a more sweeping and general version of the historical narrative that Hegel offers in his text. That sketch will reference several of the best-known discussions of the later parts of the book: Hegel's discussion of Antigone; his account of the transition from ancient Greek religion "in the form of art" to Christian, revealed religion; the descriptions of faith, the Enlightenment, and the French Revolution; and, finally, Hegel's discussion of morality. When I reference these more specific discussions in my more general argument, I provide excurses that should help to clarify these particular sections in the *Phenomenology*. But these are only excurses: readers should feel free to read or omit them as suits their own purposes. I have tried to select the historical discussions that teachers of Hegel seem most likely to assign in classes that have only a few weeks to devote to *Phenomenology*, but there are clearly many possible choices here. My goal is to allow students and teachers to read selectively from the later chapters of Hegel's book, while still offering what I hope will be a coherent argument about what those chapters are intended to accomplish as a whole.

Let's begin with a review of the argument so far. We have seen in Chapter 6 that Hegel denies the possibility of purely theoretical knowledge. On his view, what justifies a claim to describe the world is the claim's ability to explain some feature of the world better than competing claims, and a better explanation is one that resolves some dissatisfaction we have with our understanding of the world. This notion of dissatisfaction is not finally theoretical but practical, grounded in the particular interests of human beings.

So we turned in Chapter 7 to the idea of a practical interest, but there again, Hegel offers a basically skeptical account. Human beings obviously have practical interests, but when it comes to articulating which of those interests truly have value, Hegel denies that a substantive and coherent account is possible in purely practical terms, or from the pure notion of the practical self. With Kant, Hegel argues that there is no natural desire or particular interest that could claim priority over each agent's valuing herself and all other agents as free and rational; however, against Kant, he also argues that the notions of freedom and rationality have no positive content apart from the particular standards of value that agents find for themselves in particular societies and cultures. As free agents, we are always able to reject a socially given standard of value that is at odds with our freedom and our happiness, but the attempt to rise above all such standards is doomed to failure, since the content of the pure notion of free agency is merely negative, asserting nothing more than this possible rejection of any given standard of value. A truly valuable life, Hegel holds, is not one spent in endless rebellion against the idea of socially given standards of value, but is instead one in which an agent can reflectively endorse some such standards as truly her own, even though those standards (as real, substantive standards) are already present in the existing norms and practices of the agent's culture. For this reason, the notion of pure practical agency, like the notion of purely theoretical knowledge, collapses into incoherence. Just as the notion of theoretical knowledge turns out to be burdened with the practical notion of an explanatory interest, so the notion of a practical interest turns out to be burdened with a moment of theoretical knowledge, with the empirical "given" of social norms, the facticity of already existing standards of shared value.

Hegel's position thus seems to amount to this: standards of rationality, both theoretical and practical, are inevitably conditioned by social and historical standards. A claim to know something, or a claim that something is of value, is a claim that that something conforms to our norms of belief or of action, and a claim that something is a norm of belief or of action is a claim that that norm has proven itself historically superior to other, older and discarded norms. On this view, the rest of the *Phenomenology* amounts to a history of the theoretical and practical norms of Western culture, and especially of the ways they have evolved and changed. By studying this history, we can move beyond the abstract and ultimately empty notions of pure rational knowledge and pure rational agency, and we can achieve a real and detailed knowledge of the actual standards of belief and action that have come to govern our lives. On this kind of reading, the *Phenomenology's* turn to history and culture means that the properly philosophical task of the work is over. That philosophical task was to legitimate, through the skeptical arguments we have already discussed, the need for history and culture to supply what philosophy could not. But what history and culture supply is not what philosophy once promised, a fully rational account. History and culture give us standards of rationality, but not an ultimate standard of rationality of the sort philosophy once aspired to. On this kind of view, the task of Hegelian philosophy is to discredit this traditional philosophical aspiration, and to legitimate historical and cultural knowledge as being as rational as anyone could hope for. The turn to history and culture is thus justified by philosophy, but it does not provide any sort of philosophical justification of its own.

But this kind of reading – which has become especially prominent in recent Anglo-American interpretations of Hegel as "anti-metaphysical" and fully consistent with scientific naturalism – should strike us as troubling. The sharp separation of the philosophical and historical tasks of the *Phenomenology* is at odds with the apparent structure of the work, especially with the alleged progress toward "absolute knowing," which (if achieved) would seem to complete and not simply to discredit the traditional aspiration of philosophy. It looks like Hegel wants his account of history to have philosophical significance in itself, not just the significance it would have once the idea of philosophical significance had been philosophically discredited. But even if we ignore or deflate beyond recognition the aspiration to absolute knowing, Hegel's turn to history still implies that there is more philosophical work to be done. We have already seen that Hegel wants to say more than that claims to theoretical and practical rationality are appeals to existing social norms. He also wants to say that certain social norms – in particular, those of the modern West – themselves have a claim to rationality that other norms do not. It is this claim that is supposed to be justified by the appeal to history, since a Hegelian history will try to show us how the privileged social norms emerged as superior to their earlier and now historically discredited competitors. But what do terms like *superior* and *discredited* mean here? It is this question that demands more philosophical work.[1]

The answer Hegel wants to give is this one: a norm is historically vindicated if it fits better with our sense of ourselves, if we can identify with it better than with earlier norms that turned out to exhibit a kind of incoherence, a tension between the norm and our sense of ourselves as believing and acting subjects. A notion of subjectivity or identity, then, is what grounds the appeal to normative superiority: privileged norms are just those that we identify more strongly with given our cultural experience. But this again looks like too weak a claim, since different historical experiences and different cultural identities could produce very different accounts of privileged norms. To avoid this weak form of communitarianism (the result of all too many contemporary "Hegelianisms"), we need to understand that Hegel wants more out of his notion of subjectivity or identity than mere contingence on historical and cultural experience. Or, even more precisely, he thinks that the notion of contingence on historical and cultural experience itself can provide a positive content for his notion of subjectivity, so that this notion of subjectivity can itself rise above the relativity of particular histories and cultures. For all of Hegel's criticisms of Kantian formalism, there remains a kind of formalism in Hegel's own account of subjectivity: to be a subject is to struggle with the fact of one's own contingency. To be a subject is to be able to deny any particular norm, but yet to have to identify with some norms as one's own. And those norms are best, for everyone, that cohere with this fact about being a self. How can we identify those norms? Hegel's answer is: we need to look at the way human beings have struggled with the fact of their own contingency.

This struggle is really what a Hegelian history is about. The Hegelian turn to history is not simply a turn to the particular experiences of different subjects struggling with different norms. It is rather a turn to the experience of subjects struggling with the idea of normativity itself, with the limits placed on our claims to normativity by our historical and cultural specificity. Hegel is less interested in the particular developments of particular cultures than with the development of the idea of culture itself. It might seem that culture means nothing more than historical specificity, and in one sense Hegel grants that this is correct. The idea of culture itself is not historically

---

[1] See the discussion of recent analytic readings of Hegel in chapter 1, note 6. For similar concerns about this kind of reading, see Alan Patten, *Hegel's Idea of Freedom* (Oxford University Press, 1999), chapter 1, especially pp. 27–34. See also the discussion in Joshua Foa Dienstag, "What Is Living and What Is Dead in the Interpretation of Hegel," *Political Theory* 29:2 (2001), pp. 262–275.

specific, but for that very reason, it seems to lack any particular content. There would seem to be no escape from this dilemma of relativism and empty formalism, but Hegel thinks we can find one if we turn to the history of the idea of culture itself. That history will concern not particular cultures but culture in general, but precisely because it is also a real history of real cultural developments, it will have positive content. Hence it is wrong to see the *Phenomenology*'s turn to history and culture as a turn away from traditional philosophical tasks. Hegel's interest in the history of culture, as a history of the idea of culture, is really a philosophical examination and (if successful) a vindication of the idea of culture itself.

TWO SENSES OF CULTURE

We can start to get at the way the idea of culture binds the work of history and philosophy together if we think about the two ways we tend to use the word *culture*. In both cases, culture is contrasted with nature, but the contrasts are quite different, and that difference itself implies a kind of philosophical problem.

On the one hand, something is cultural if it cannot be understood in the way we understand the rest of nature, through a merely physical or biological description. Something is cultural if its "nature" cannot be fully understood without understanding the contribution of socialization, the process by which particular groups of human beings impose particular meanings and purposes on particular objects. As Rousseau and many others have emphasized, what makes human beings cultural and not just natural beings is the symbolic capacity inherent in our use of language, which infuses arbitrary sounds and markings with particular meanings, meanings that can only be understood through an acquaintance with the practices of particular social groups. In this sense, culture is just the imposition of new and arbitrary meanings on natural objects. Such impositions may, of course, facilitate natural ends: for example, forks, menus, and credit cards all make it easier for us to eat. In this sense, a naturalistic account of culture is possible, and it is certainly right to say that it is a part of our biological nature to have the capacity for culture. But even if we grant a fully naturalistic account of culture, even if our cultural products can be entirely explained as serving natural ends, it remains the case that those natural ends are served by means that cannot themselves be explained naturalistically – even if the means serve the ends in a highly efficient manner. In every cultural object, there remains an arbitrary symbolic element imposed through socialization. Forks, menus, and credit cards do make it easier for us to eat, but they are objects to eat and pay with only because particular societies have defined them in that way. Culture may serve nature, but only by imposing a socially dictated form onto some piece of nature.[2]

On the other hand, we also speak of culture as not just a departure from nature, but also as a development that is somehow deeper and better than nature, a development that takes human beings beyond basic physical pleasures toward higher, deeper, and more meaningful ends. This is the sense in which art, music, and literature are described as forms of culture. What is paradigmatic in these activities is not their arbitrary symbolic content (even though they might depend on our symbolic capacity) or their dependence on socialization (even though the activities can flourish only in a social context). Instead something is cultural in this second sense if it is "uplifting" or educational in the fully positive sense, opening the person who participates in the activities (even as a spectator) to a deeper and better sort of life.[3]

These two senses of culture imply two very different normative attitudes toward the idea of culture or, perhaps even more precisely, two very different attitudes toward the notion of normativity itself. For culture is what makes normativity possible, and norms themselves are just cultural standards of admirable behavior. On the second understanding of culture, our attitude toward these normative standards must be highly positive: culture makes a truly human and truly valuable life possible. But on the first understanding of culture, our attitude toward normative standards must be highly skeptical: cultural standards are always just arbitrarily imposed by socialization, and that socialization could just as easily be destructive as valuable. Which of these understandings is correct? On Hegel's view, both are right, in their own ways: human beings are nothing without the norms that culture makes possible, but at the same time, norms are arbitrary social impositions that potentially threaten the freedom and the happiness of particular human beings. So the task is not to deny either of these understandings but to find some way of reconciling them.

One familiar strategy is the utilitarian one (characteristic of most if not all naturalistic interpretations of culture). On this kind of view, norms are arbitrarily imposed, but they can also be shown to promote the general happiness and well-being of human societies over the long term. But this

[2] For an extended discussion of these matters, see John Searle, *The Construction of Social Reality* (Free Press, 1997).

[3] For a classic account of culture in this sense, see Friedrich Schiller, *On the Aesthetic Education of Man in a Series of Letters*, eds. Elizabeth M. Wilkinson and L. A. Willoughby (Oxford University Press), 2005.

kind of approach faces at least two serious problems. First, it gives us no confidence in any particular social norm, since on this kind of view, society is engaged in a lengthy evolutionary, experimental process to determine which norm works best, and we cannot be sure that any particular norm represents the end of that process. We can tell stories about why certain norms seem best, why they have evolved in the right way, but it is hard to accept these stories as finally justified without some sort of more general faux-Darwinian optimism about the tendency of the evolutionary process to produce positive outcomes. And that leads to the second problem with the approach: to accept it, we have to identify with the Darwinian ends of nature, which seem at odds with the deeper aspirations promised by the second understanding of culture. If culture exists to promote the ends of nature, then it would seem that the point of culture is to maximize the future existence of certain genetic types, and this seems far short of what we want out of a justification of culture. (It is worth noting that the most sophisticated of utilitarian writers, John Stuart Mill, endorses nothing like this view; his doctrine of higher pleasures breaks sharply with the premises of this approach.[4])

If we set aside the claim that cultural norms simply promote natural ends, ends that we already have, we need some other way of affirming that the cultural norms are truly ours, even though they have simply been imposed on us through socialization. Here it is important to see that the problem is not the fact of socialization in itself (it is not very difficult to accept that complicated or "advanced" cultural norms may first have to be introduced by a kind of imposition), but rather the lingering worry that the fact of socialization may make it impossible for us to say that our identification with the norms should count as rational, since that identification might itself be nothing more than an artifact of the socialization process. To overcome this kind of skeptical worry, we need some way of understanding the moment of seemingly arbitrary socialization as not just necessary for the transmission of particular norms, but also as necessary for any sort of rational acceptance at all. But what kind of necessity could this be? Hegel's answer is that the necessity is historical: our very notions of rational acceptance have emerged through a historical process in which the notion of culture, in both of its potentially conflicting senses, has played a central role. Since our history, the particular cultural legacy we have been given, includes this struggle to clarify the notion of rational acceptance through a struggle with the notion of culture itself, we can say that the particularity

---

[4] John Stuart Mill, *Utilitarianism*, chapter 2.

of our cultural experience is not just an arbitrary imposition, but also something we can affirm as necessarily rational, because it is necessary for our sense of ourselves as rational.

We said at the start of this section that for Hegel, the notion of culture binds the work of history and philosophy together in a special way. We are now in a position to better understand how this is so. The notion of culture introduces a philosophical problem: how can we affirm the cultural norms we have been socialized to accept as rational, particularly if even the standards we use to affirm anything may themselves be culturally imposed? This problem looks intractable unless it turns out that our cultural experience itself includes a way of getting beyond this problem, a way of seeing the problem not as an obstacle but as something necessary for our sense of ourselves. The philosophical problem of culture is thus addressed by a history of Western ideas of culture, which will show the philosophical worry about cultural particularity to be both our particular historical inheritance and necessary for anything we could count as a rational acceptance as a cultural norm. The philosophical problem of culture is a problem about historical contingency, and since that contingency cannot be eliminated, the task is to find a way of seeing our history as something more than mere contingency. Hegel's claim is that his history of Western culture can do exactly that. If this history can in fact allow us to cope with the problem of culture, a problem that everyone can be taken to have, then that history will not just be a particular or merely Western history, but a history that is somehow relevant to everyone.

THE GREEK WORLD AND ITS FRAGMENTATION

Hegel's history of Western culture, as presented not just in the *Phenomenology* but also in later works like the *Philosophy of History,* is extraordinarily more detailed, more complex, and more interesting than anything that can be described in a brief work like this. There are also important changes in Hegel's views over time. Nonetheless there remains a basic pattern to Hegel's history, a pattern that remains unchanged. It is this pattern that I will examine here, despite the inevitable losses and distortions that will result from such a brief and schematic account.

In a view that borrows heavily from earlier German Romantic writers, a view that we have already discussed in Chapter 1, Hegel holds that Western culture began with the ancient Greeks, and that Greek culture offers us a glimpse of an especially beautiful and especially harmonious life, a kind of culture that is now irretrievably lost to us. Compared to his Romantic predecessors, Hegel is far less nostalgic about the loss of this Greek culture, far less disappointed by the modern world, and far less willing to distort Greek thinking to preserve the illusion of a harmony. Indeed Hegel often seems to think that the ideal Greek culture was lost even as it was theorized in Greek writing and works of art, that its possibility was doomed almost from the start. But even this way of talking still assumes the vision of a lost, even if always already lost, cultural harmony. On this kind of vision, the Greeks agreed on a view of what made a human life worthwhile, and expressed this view in their art and in their literature.[5] Here it is easiest to work with the basic image of a Homeric warrior-hero: a person physically gifted and hence also physically beautiful, and at the same time a person who fights cleverly and courageously in defense of his *polis,* and hence also morally admirable. What is less important here is less the particular virtues embodied in the notion of the Greek hero – as Athenian political institutions became more democratic, the capacity for persuasive public argument became more important than simple decisive leadership – but rather the general conception of the hero who, by embodying those virtues, is both an exceptional human being and the person who embodies human characteristics most fully. A version of this view persists all the way to Aristotle: virtue is especially admirable behavior, but it is also simply the right exercise of our natural human capacities, now most prominently not our skills in physical combat but rather our capacities for rational deliberation and choice. On this kind of view, nature provides us with certain basic human capacities, and exercising those capacities fully is excellent or admirable behavior. Human culture, our social and political institutions, exist to help us develop these capacities; thus nature, culture, and individual human beings have exactly the same end: the achievement of human excellence. It is this supposed consensus among nature, culture, and the individual that constitutes the special harmony of the Greek understanding of the world.

For Hegel, this kind of view was exploded by the appearance of dissenting individuals who questioned whether received cultural norms really did represent true human excellence, and who were willing to persist in their own valuations even at the risk of social persecution. Thus Hegel's history of Greek culture pays very little attention to Aristotle and a great deal of attention to Sophocles and to Plato, who, in their depictions of dissenters like Antigone and Socrates, describe individuals deeply committed to ethical norms, each claiming to be faithful to nature and to divine commands,

---

[5] For more on Hegel's account of Greek culture, see Terry Pinkard, *Hegel's Phenomenology: The Sociality of Reason* (Cambridge University Press, 1994), pp. 135–146.

who nonetheless come into conflict with the standards of their societies and, when they willingly violated those standards, were punished with death. If the sort of harmony just described were actual, these things could not happen; in showing that they could, Sophocles and Plato raised the question of whether Greek societies had any stable and coherent account of what norms were truly admirable, and truly in conformity with our nature. On the classically Greek conception we have described, good action consists in fidelity to cultural norms, and heroic action consists in just the same sort of fidelity, although that fidelity requires unwavering commitment and physical risk. The heroism of Antigone and Socrates, by contrast, is shown precisely in their commitment to defy cultural expectations, to refuse to do what authority demands. Of course both Antigone and Socrates take themselves to be adhering to cultural norms: Antigone is obeying the gods and displaying loyalty to her dead brother, and in describing himself as a kind of gadfly in the *Apology*, Socrates even presents himself as a kind of good Athenian democrat. But in their professed fidelity to norms of good behavior, Antigone and Socrates are no different from their opponents, from Creon and Meletus, each of whom has familiar and coherent – even if not entirely convincing – accounts of why their actions are simply those of recognizably good political agents. What sets Antigone and Socrates apart is not their commitment to cultural norms, but the special way they maintain this commitment in the face of cultural scorn. As the citizens of Thebes recoil at his harsh punishment of a woman, Creon too begins to describe himself as heroic in just this way, for remaining steadfast in his commitment to the law. (Since Meletus never appears or presents himself in this sort of light, it is hard to admire him in any way.) And it is ethical commitment itself, Hegel maintains, that brings about the destruction of the Greek ethical world.

Excursus 1: Antigone

On Hegel's famous reading, Sophocles' play *Antigone* dramatizes this break-down of Greek ethical life, which first appears as a kind of immediate harmony between the individual and the social order: "the *ethical life* of a nation in so far as it is the *immediate truth* – the individual that is a world" (441).[6] Within this harmony, there is no conflict between existing social

---

[6] Hegel's reading of *Antigone* has been enormously influential and has inspired countless responses. For an important account of the reception of the play and Hegel's contribution to it, see George Steiner, *Antigones* (Yale University Press, 1998). Hegel's claims about Antigone as a woman have prompted

norms ("the *realm of culture,* in the harsh reality of its objective element") and the individual's own commitments (the *world of belief or faith,* the *realm of essential being*" [442]). This division, however, is always potentially present in the Greek or any other conception of ethical life, and it becomes explicit in self-conscious ethical action. "*Action* divides it into substance, and consciousness of the substance; and divides the substance as well as consciousness" (444). An agent who conceives of herself as acting ethically, as Antigone does, takes herself to be following norms that have a special status, and this special status ("the inner Notion or general possibility of the ethical sphere in general" [450]) can be distinguished from the specific dictates of particular social norms ("the *known* law, and the prevailing custom" [448]). This distinction does not always have to lead to conflict, but a self-conscious ethical agent cannot regard the mere existence of a custom or law as providing a justification for ethical conformity to the law. In that sense, the conflict between Antigone and Creon is already implicit in any case of ethical action; the ethical agent is always siding with a deeper ethical justification, a kind of divine law that is prior to and ought to ground the positive, humanly created laws of the state or the community.

The divine law, says Hegel, has a natural existence; it has a permanence that stands in contrast to the artificial, mutable standards of human legislators. But as a law of ethics, the divine law applies not to inorganic nature or to the lower animals, but only to relationships between human beings. The divine law is thus the law of the natural human community, the family. Even within the family, though, not every relationship is ethical, "for the ethical relationship is intrinsically universal" (451). Specific attachments based on affection for particular individuals do not count as universal in this sense: "the ethical connection between the members of the Family is not that of feeling, or the relationship of love" (451). The ethical content of the family must be found in duties to the family as a whole, or to particular members of the family only insofar as they are members of the family. But to a very great extent, the family exists to care for its children when they are young and vulnerable, and to equip them with the knowledge that they will need to navigate the world. In this sense, the family exists not for its own ends, but to prepare its children to live on their own in the world beyond the family. It is life in the larger society, not anything about the family

---

a great deal of criticism from feminist readers, many of whom want to use those claims as a basis for a more generalized critique of Hegel's thought grounded in French post-structuralism: Lacan, Derrida, and Irigiray have all written influentially on this part of Hegel. For a recent account from this point of view, see Judith Butler, *Antigone's Claim* (Columbia University Press, 2002).

itself, that is the end of parenting. "This determination does not fall within the Family itself, but bears on what is truly universal, the community; it has, rather, a negative relation to the Family, and consists in expelling the community from the Family, subduing the natural aspect and separateness of his existence, and training him to be virtuous, to a life in and for the universal." So once again we have failed to locate the particular ethical end of the family; the care and education of the individual is really the end of the community, of the human and not the divine law. "But because it is only as a citizen that he is actual and substantial, the individual, so far as he is not a citizen but belongs to the Family, is only an unreal impotent shadow" (451).

The individual is thus most truly a member of the family, in the purely ethical and universal sense, not as a child, when he is in training for citizenship, nor as an adult, when he is in fact a citizen, but only when he is no longer capable of citizenship and has become, from the existing community's point of view, "an unreal important shadow": that is, when he is dead. The death of the individual is in itself the action of nature, which undermines the physical workings of his body and disperses its component parts back into the rest of nature. In the physical destruction of the body, the individual is reduced to nothingness. Only the family, says Hegel, can rescue the dead individual and proclaim, against the verdicts of nature and the community, that he still has meaning and value. "The Family keeps away from the dead this dishonoring of him by unconscious appetites and abstract entities, and puts its own action in their place, and weds the blood-relation to the bosom of the earth, to the elemental imperishable individuality. The Family thereby makes him a member of a community which prevails over and holds under control the forces of particular material elements and the lower forms of life, which sought to unloose themselves against him and to destroy him" (452). On this reading, Antigone's insistence that her brother Polynices be buried, no matter whether his conduct or his burial violated the law of the state, becomes the clearest example of the ethics of the family, "the perfect *divine* law, or the positive *ethical* action towards the individual" (453). Hegel even has a story about why it is a sister's burial of her brother that best dramatizes this kind of ethical relationship. The relationship between a husband and a wife is colored with affection and sexual desire (457); that between a parent and a child is, again, oriented toward education and future citizenship (456). The relationship between siblings, by contrast, is neither sexual nor educative; it a pure expression of the familial bond (457). Since this bond is most clearly expressed in the family's reclaiming of the dead body of the individual who is no longer capable of a role in the adult community, it is best expressed in the desire of a woman (the traditional representative of the domestic world) to bury a man (the traditional inhabitant of the public world of citizenship). Upon his death, Antigone must see that Polynices returns home from the male realm of activity and public legislation, and passes safely into the care of the gods, women, and ethical permanence (457–459).

At the same time, Polynices' crime against the state, his revolt against the rule of his brother Eteocles, stands as a symbol of the contingent and hence always potentially arbitrary character of positive law. As brothers and heirs of Oedipus, Polynices and Eteocles had an "equal right" to kingship: "the inequality of the earlier and the later birth, an inequality which is a natural difference, has no importance for them when they enter the ethical life of the community" (473). Still, Thebes needed a single ruler: the state "does not tolerate a duality of individuality; and the ethical necessity of this unity is confronted with the natural accident of there being more than one" (473). Thus there arose the generic, mechanical, and thus arbitrary solution of having the brothers share the kingship by turns. What placed Polynices and not Eteocles in the political wrong is not that he desired to rule, nor that he was unqualified to rule, nor even that he fought to rule; in all of these respects, the brothers were exactly the same. Polynices' crime consisted simply in his not having, by the luck of the draw, the throne at the time the civil war began (473). Mere possession of the throne is also all that justifies Creon in his punishment of Antigone; she and everyone else ought to respect his decree simply because he has made it. Creon attacks both Polynices and Antigone as renegade individuals who threaten the common life of the city, who value their own private ends over the public good (473, 475). But his own rule turns out to be just the same sort of assertion of private will; his failure to offer any further justification for his decree means that it lacks the ethical power inherent in the idea of the divine law (474) and substitutes for this power the force of his own individuality (475).

Once the law of the community is exposed as an arbitrary convention, there remains only the ethical individual and her own commitment to the right. In this respect, as we have already noted, Antigone and Creon are entirely alike: they are both fully convinced that they are morally required to act as they do, and this consciousness is precisely what both allows and insists that they violate other, wholly familiar norms of conduct. Their ethical commitment (466) is at the same time the source of their ethical failings, for as Hegel points out, one is truly guilty of a crime if one consciously and intentionally violates a law (468). In the strength of their commitment, though, the positive character of particular norms comes to nothing. In the Greek ethical world, agents' commitment to norms is "essentially *immediate*" (476); individuals simply identify with norms as serving their own ends. The paradox of this immediate commitment is that truly committed individuals expose existing norms as standing in radical need of justification; the strength of their ethical commitment can find no clear expression beyond the assertion of their own consciences. "[N]ow the *living* Spirits of the nation succumb through their own individuality and perish in a *universal* community, whose simple universality is soulless and dead, and is alive only in the *single* individual, *qua* single. The ethical shape of Spirit has vanished and another takes its place" (475).

What the stories of Antigone and Socrates do is to drive a wedge between the idea of shared cultural norms, on the one hand, and the idea of ethical commitment on the other. Instead of merely embodying or committing themselves to acknowledged norms in a fuller or deeper way, the ethical individual is now a solitary, marginalized figure whose commitment to norms is ignored or even criticized by his or her culture. On a social level, the result of this new conception of ethical individuality is just the ending of the stories of Antigone and Socrates: the tragic fate of the dissenter is to suffer persecution and even death. In Sophocles' telling, there remains the sense that this fate is, in some sense, the solitary ethical individual's own doing; it is part of the tragedy of Antigone and Creon that they each adopt a perversely solitary account of ethical behavior, so that their commitments are as self-destructive as they are morally admirable. But in Plato's account of Socrates' trial and death, this kind of reading is pushed to the side; the responsibility for the execution is placed entirely on the Athenian society that failed to recognize Socrates' ethical commitment. (Plato seems to blame Socrates only for political naïveté, and perhaps not even for that.) What makes this Platonic reading possible is that Socrates' ethical commitment is just to philosophical questioning, to the rational examination of cultural norms. What makes the solitary ethical individual valuable is that someone like Socrates, and only someone like Socrates, is needed to ask if the cultural norms we have been given really do have value. On this kind of view, the solitary ethical individual, whatever his or her social fate, is of ultimate value, because he or she embodies the commitment to freedom and rationality – not simply submitting to cultural norms, but asking first whether those norms are truly of value. It is this commitment to rational examination – and not any particular norm that a solitary ethical individual claims to uphold – that Hegel understands as emerging from the stories of Antigone and Socrates. On the one hand, those stories describe the breakdown of Greek culture, the loss of faith in a single set of norms. On the other hand, the product of that breakdown is philosophy, understood as the demand that all norms submit themselves to critical scrutiny. While the ethical burden was once on the individual to conform to privileged norms, after Socrates the burden is now on the culture and its norms to conform to the rational demands of the inquiring individual.

So what norms could conform to those demands? In Plato and all the way through Hellenistic philosophy, the favored answer consists in a kind of philosophical formalism: the norms that philosophy prefers are precisely those that encourage and enable philosophical activity. Thus in the *Republic,* Plato argues both that the best life is one spent doing philosophy, and that the just society is organized around norms that allow philosophical activity to flourish. But what justifies the leap from the claim that philosophical questioning is good, that norms require rational justification, to the conclusion that philosophical activity is the highest form of life? Why argue that the result of philosophical questioning will be the vindication of philosophical activity itself? Greek philosophy seems to offer two possible answers. First, there is the Platonic view that philosophical questioning is inherently connected to the pursuit of Forms, pure theoretical objects of knowledge that also are of ultimate beauty and value. We have already seen, in Chapter 6, that Hegel rejects this kind of view as empty. Second, there is the Hellenistic view that philosophical activity is valuable not because it reaches a purely theoretical goal, but because there is a kind of ultimate happiness in questioning and thus rising above the objects and activities of the ordinary world. But as we have seen in our discussion of Stoicism and skepticism in Chapter 7, Hegel sees this kind of view not as a positive achievement of an essential practical interest, but merely an escape from or a denial of what is supposed to be inessential, the ordinary interests and norms of the existing social world. For Hegel, Greek philosophical formalism is empty in both its theoretical and its practical forms, and ancient philosophy ends in the disappointed conclusion that no form of life, no cultural norm, could be adequate to the ultimate rational demands of the solitary ethical individual.

On Hegel's view, the pure expression of this demand, expressed only as demand, is Christianity. The rise of the Christian religion accompanied the decline of Greek and Roman thinking, Hegel argues, because Christianity expressed exactly this decline. On Hegel's account, Christianity proclaims the infinite worth of each individual, solely as individual, and proclaims the circumstances and institutions of the actual world to be too corrupt to sustain the moral and spiritual promise inherent in the idea of individual worth. But against the Hellenistic view, which sought only escape from this world, Christianity holds out – though only in paradoxical and hence inexplicable form – the promise of a world redeemed, a God in physical and human form, the bare idea that there could be a human way of life that matched the absolute ethical and rational demands with which Socrates (and now Jesus) confronted human culture. Christianity does not itself provide a new form of culture; rather it assures the ultimate fragmentation of ancient culture by raising the idea of the solitary ethical individual, and the idea that the culture is inadequate to the demands of that individual, to the status of absolute principles. In the story of Jesus, Christianity promises to reconcile these principles, but as a form of pure faith that cannot be rationally articulated, it offers nothing more than the hope for reconciliation, not a reconciliation itself.

Excursus 2: Religion

In Hegel's history of religion, Christianity stands at the end of a long process of historical development through which the rational core of religious expression is supposedly clarified, and so the Christian tradition is assigned a position of superiority over all other traditions. At times the superiority of Christianity is exchanged for the superiority of rational reflection: both the inferior and the superior forms of religion are said to be found in all traditions, and the development of religion's rational core is understood as a universal, ecumenical process (684). As is typical of such claims for the superiority of a particular tradition, or for the essential identity of all traditions, Hegel's arguments do not reflect any sort of thorough engagement with non-Western religious traditions like Buddhism or Hinduism, or even with other Western religious traditions like Judaism or Islam. The *Phenomenology*'s chapter on religion is not really a history of religion in general; the only traditions that receive close analysis are the ancient Greek and the Christian. It is thus best to understand Hegel as describing a very specific part of the history of religion: the process by which the Roman world abandoned Greek paganism in favor of Christianity. It is this process, Hegel thinks, that can be understood as a kind of rational development, through which the essential nature of religion can finally be understood.[7]

---

[7] In treating Hegel's chapter on religion at this point, I am, for the only time in this book, altering the order of Hegel's presentation for purposes of my own. In the text of the *Phenomenology*, the account of the history of religion I discuss here occurs after the account of modernity I discuss later. The section on "Religion" occurs after the section on "Morality," not the other way around. So I need to explain my reasons for treating them in reverse order.

My main goal here is to preserve the historical sequence of Hegel's account, to present the whole of the later parts of the *Phenomenology* as a single historical narrative that runs from ancient Greece to

Three main assumptions guide this account. First, Hegel assumes that religion is always an attempt to find in the world an expression of a higher, divine power. Second, Hegel assumes that this search for the divine is driven by something in us as human beings. And third, Hegel assumes that this religious drive in us is itself the proper object of religious faith, the true expression of the divine. In that sense, the progressive development of religion is one that moves from external to internal expressions of religion, from the enchantment of the world to the sacralization of inner experience.

In what Hegel understands as the earliest and simplest form of religion, natural religion, the believer attempts to locate in natural phenomena themselves the expression of divine power. The first candidate for this expression is light, the natural force that allows us to recognize everything for what it is, as opposed to the all-consuming void of darkness (685–686). But the pure simplicity of light lacks any determinate meaning or content, so natural religion must look instead to the specific features of nature that are more than simply there, those that seem to exist for a purpose. These are living things, which grow and develop according to their own purposes. This kind of worship takes as its object either plants, which for Hegel are too passive to count as sources of significance, or animals, whose activity is nonetheless exhausted by their struggles with one another to survive (689). The activity of nature is not enough to suggest what Hegel thinks the religious believer is looking for, which is the idea of a power that is itself higher than nature. Such a power would shape the objects of nature to its own purposes, and that idea is expressed not by the generation and decay of plants and animals, but in the conscious shaping of objects by a conscious being. This is what Hegel calls an artificer (690–691), and to the extent that the product of the artificer is supposed to express nothing more than the artificer's power as a creator and shaper of objects, that product is a work of art. For a work

---

modern Europe. Hegel's aim is to provide such a single narrative, even if he understands it as having several dimensions. And it is clear that he sees this narrative as culminating in modernity: even in the actual sequence of the text of the *Phenomenology*, there is a clear narrative culmination in the account of forgiveness that ends in paragraph 671. From a narrative point of view, the succeeding chapters on "Religion" and "Absolute Knowing" are only retrospective reflections on what this narrative culmination amounts to. In my view, the section on religion is placed after the account of morality because it might not be clear to the modern European reader that the moment of reconciliation that Hegel finds in modernity really amounts to a fulfillment of the Christian religious tradition. Modernity looks too secular for that, and it is exactly this skepticism that I think Hegel wants to address, after the fact. Even in my own account, I include a later discussion of the paradox inherent in Hegel's account of modernity and religion – i.e., that the secularization characteristic of modernity finally helps to realize and not to undermine the Christian faith.

Of course, since my discussion of religion is presented here as yet another excursus, there is nothing to prevent the reader or instructor who wants to preserve the sequence of Hegel's text from reading or assigning this excursus at a later point.

of art is an artifact that exists not for any external purpose, but solely to display the creative power of the artist.

What Hegel thinks is distinctive about ancient Greek religion is that it self-consciously identifies works of art not just as vehicles of religious expression, but also as in some sense the objects of religious expression. Greek religion, Hegel tells us, is "religion in the form of art." This is a highly idiosyncratic interpretation of Greek religious practice, in which epic poetry and tragedy are regarded as deeper forms of religiosity than sacrifices to Zeus. But Hegel goes even further: the works of Homer and Sophocles are not finally homages to the pagan gods but substitutes for them. What is worshipped in religion in the form of art is the power of the divine, characterized specifically as the divine power of artistic expression. On this view, Hegel's modern, Christian understanding of the ancient, pagan gods as mythical does not present the usual obstacles to entering into the religious perspective of the Greeks, because it is precisely as mythical, human creations that the stories of the Greek gods are said to have religious power.

The most basic expressions of religion in the form of art are the simplest and most abstract, which represent nothing more than the power of the artist to shape objects, and which therefore take the form of simple shapes (705–706). But in a repetition of the evolution of the forms of natural religion, the simple and hence muted forms of abstract art give way to stories of the forces of nature, which themselves evolve to more closely resemble and concern themselves with the actions of human beings. This is the victory of the Greek gods over their ancestors, who recede into the background of inert nature, the "chaotic being and confused strife of the freely existing elements, the unethical realm of the Titans" (707). But the Greek gods still stand apart from their human creators, the real source of religious power: "The artist, then, learns in his work that he did not produce a being *like himself*" (709). What follows is a process in which the gods draw ever closer to human beings: first by communicating particular messages, delivered by oracles (712–713), and then by imparting to particular human beings the power of the divine, in the ecstatic energies of the cult (714–715). The cult is a "living work of art"; rather than trying to embody the divine in some created object, its members claim to embody the divine in themselves. But this is only a claim: we can only look at the ecstasies of cults, like the abilities of oracles, as secret powers, unverifiable and inexplicable to anyone, even the oracles and cult members themselves (716). The cult represents only the idea of the divine speaking through the human. What is required is not that the divine is expressed to or through the human, but that it is revealed as human experience itself, in the actions of a human being. This human being is the hero of the epic, whose adventures represent the story of a single individual whose story nonetheless embraces the whole range of peoples and gods:

The business which is the object of these general exertions has two sides: the side of the *self*, by which the business is accomplished by a totality of actual nations and the individualities standing at their head; and the side of the *universal*, by which it is accomplished by their substantial powers . . . The universal powers have the form of individuality and hence the principle of action in them; what they effect appears, therefore, to proceed entirely from them and to be as free an action as that of men. Consequently, both gods and men have done one and the same thing . . . Ephemeral mortals who as nothing are at the same time the mighty *self* that brings into subjection the universal Beings, offends the gods, and, in general, procures for them an actual existence and an interest in acting. Just as, conversely, these impotent universal Beings who nourish themselves on the gifts of men and through them alone get something to do, are the natural substance and the material of all events, and are equally the ethical matter and the "pathos" of action. (730)

In the Epic, what is described is not the gods or human beings, but rather the actions of human beings insofar as they are also the actions of the gods. It is, therefore, a "spiritual work of art," not simply the artist's trying to embody the divine in some created object or claiming to embody the divine in himself. The epic hero, as he comes to life in the telling of his story, is the human embodiment of the divine. As for the artist, the "minstrel" or singer of the epic poem, he erases himself in the successful telling of his tale: "He is the organ that vanishes in its content; what counts is not his own self but his Muse, the universal song" (729).

But to truly erase himself, and to eliminate the separation between the teller of the tale and the hero he is describing, the teller must become the hero, and that can only happen in drama, where the actor does not describe but takes on the role of the hero: "these characters *exist* as actual human beings who impersonate the heroes and portray them, not in the form of a narrative, but in the actual speech of the actors themselves" (733). Still, the performance is not simply the hero's actions; it is those actions displayed before the spectators of the play, who can only look on. Tragedy internalizes their perspective, the "spectator-consciousness" within the play itself, in the group character of the chorus, who comment on the fate of the hero but have no power to affect it. In this sense, the chorus of spectators are inessential, but that assumes that the hero's essentiality is real – that is, that his claim to represent the divine will is justified. And that claim, Hegel thinks, is just what tragedy is set up to question. The hero believes that he is acting rightly, and thus carrying out the will of the gods (or, in the case of Oedipus, avoiding the claims of the gods), and thereby ends up acting wrongly, and thereby assuring that the heretofore unknown but true will of the gods is finally carried out. "He who was able to unlock the riddle of the Sphinx, and he who trusted with childlike confidence, are both sent to destruction through what the god revealed to them" (737). The ineffectuality of the chorus turns out to be their essential knowledge. Because they lack the self-confident commitments of the hero, they are unable to act, but also able to see the way in which these commitments are the source of the hero's downfall. The hero is in fact the instrument of the gods, but not in the way he understood himself to be. The separation between the human and the divine thus persists even in tragedy, and in fact what tragedy turns out to dramatize is not the embodiment of the divine in the human, but the falsehood of any human claim to embody the divine.

But once this lesson is isolated, the claim to divine wisdom looks ridiculous, and tragedy is converted into comedy (744). With the action of tragedy, the hero is still the favored individual of the gods, but once he is reduced to nothingness, there remain only the spectators, isolated from the gods but secure in the wisdom that they know nothing. They now see that the tragic hero knows just as little of what the gods want as they do. He is just one of them, no different from the spectators, and in that thought, tragedy loses its power. The spectators know the actor who plays the hero to be just a man, and they demand that he remove his actor's mask, so that the audience can see him in his ordinariness (742–743). In comedy, the claim to divine wisdom is still on display, but it now appears as the risible attempts of human beings to attain a superior wisdom. All that is left is the attempt of human beings to rise above themselves, to show themselves as capable of embodying the divine. That, in the end, was what religion as art was all about, from the start:

The *individual self* is the negative power through which and in which the gods, as also their moments, viz. existent nature and the thoughts of their specific characters, vanish. At the same time, the individual self is not the emptiness of this disappearance but, on the contrary, preserves itself in this very nothingness, abides with itself and is the sole actuality. In it, the religion of art is consummated and has completely returned into itself. Through the fact that it is the individual consciousness in the certainty of itself that exhibits itself as this absolute power, this latter has lost the form of something *presented to consciousness*, something altogether *separate* from *consciousness* and alien to it, as it were the statue, and also the living beautiful corporeality, or the content of the epic and the powers and the persons of tragedy. (747)

This individual self is, once again, an isolated individual, capable of ethical commitment and spiritual longing but, as a finite and limited individual, bound to specific forms of life and standards of value that do not necessarily conform to its absolute ethical and spiritual demands. The failure of these demands is what Hegel has already called the Unhappy Consciousness: "the tragic fate of the certainty of self that aims to be absolute. It is the consciousness of the loss of all *essential* being in the *certainty of itself*, and of the loss even of this knowledge about itself – the loss of substance as well as of the self, it is the grief which expresses itself in the hard saying that 'God is dead'" (752).

The death of God, of course, is in another sense the very symbol of Christianity, and like Kierkegaard after him, Hegel affirms a connection between the atheist's claim that human beings stand alone, apart from any god, and the Christian's claim that God died on the cross for our sins. The utter separation of human and divine is what, for both Hegel and Kierkegaard, gives Christianity its symbolic power. That power comes from the transformation of human finitude into its opposite:

The death of the divine Man, as death, is abstract negativity, the immediate result of the movement which ends only in natural universality. Death loses this natural meaning in spiritual self-consciousness, i.e. it comes to be its just stated Notion; death becomes transfigured from its immediate meaning, viz. the non-being of this particular individual, into the universality of the Spirit who dwells in His community, dies in it every day, and is daily resurrected. (784)

That God would take on fully human form and die, that He would experience the very finitude that thwarts our higher aspirations, and yet that this death would itself symbolize the realization of those aspirations – this is exactly what the Unhappy Consciousness thinks it cannot have. What Kierkegaard calls the paradox of Christianity – that God would become human so that humans can become divine – is for Hegel a non-rational solution to the problem that Hegel identifies as definitively rational: how to show that human, cultural standards of value can have a kind of ultimate justification. The Christian believer cannot solve that problem rationally; the believer's commitment is simply a faith that the problem can be solved, that the ethical and spiritual longings of the individual human self can, despite all appearances, be satisfied.[8]

---

[8] For more on Hegel's account of religion, see Emil Fackenheim, *The Religious Dimension in Hegel's Thought* (University of Chicago Press, 1982); Charles Taylor, *Hegel* (Cambridge University Press, 1975), pp. 197–213 and 480–509; Terry Pinkard, *Hegel's Phenomenology*, pp. 221–260; and Laurence

Hegel's account of Christianity, with its emphases on the purity of faith and the solitude of the individual, may seem historically jarring: more Protestant than Catholic, seeming to anticipate the radical Lutheranism of Kierkegaard more than it describes the actual beginnings of Christian practice. In itself, the criticism is accurate, but it also obscures a crucial feature of Hegelian historical narrative. When he discusses a cultural phenomenon like Christianity, Hegel is not concerned to describe it in its place and time, but rather to explain the meaning that it has for us now, looking back from our position in the present. In this sort of exercise, historical explanation does not need to strip away the thoughts and events of intervening years in order to recover the truth of the past. Rather, those intervening thoughts and events might well help us to understand the essence of the historical phenomenon – provided that we can, looking backward with the aid of those thoughts and events, tell a more coherent and recognizable story about why the phenomenon was distinctive (which, it is important to add, is all that understanding "the essence" of a historical phenomenon amounts to in any case). So although actual Christian practice, especially throughout the history of medieval Europe, may have been tied far more closely to communal practices and norms than Hegel's account would suggest, Hegel's argument is rather that what makes Christianity distinctive, what distinguishes it more clearly from pagan and especially from Greek thinking, is its emphasis on faith and the solitary individual. Protestantism, on this view, represents a kind of clarification of Christianity, an isolation of its distinctive elements. If this clarification turns out to be influenced by some distinctly modern phenomena – most obviously the materialism of Galilean and Newtonian physics and the secularism of modern political states, which drove religion to the private realm of the individual's own convictions – that is not, for Hegel, any kind of embarrassment for his account. Rather, the isolation of Christian faith in the sphere of individual conviction is precisely what enables us to understand what is distinctive about Christianity, what has not been obscured or swept away by intervening developments.

MODERNITY AS RECONCILIATION

Indeed, a crucial and paradoxical feature of Hegel's view is that the modern world is more Christian precisely because it is less Christian, because the

Dickey, "Hegel on Religion and Philosophy," in Frederick Beiser (ed.), *The Cambridge Companion to Hegel* (Cambridge University Press, 1993), pp. 301–347.

distinctiveness of Christian faith is brought out by the secularism of the modern world, which insists that Christianity is nothing but pure faith. But what is even more paradoxical is that Hegel's view does not stop here. He argues that precisely because modern secularism treats Christianity merely as faith, the modern world must regard Christian conviction as basically unjustified, as lacking the material and hence rational grounding claimed by physics and secular politics. In this way, Christianity is reduced to nothing more than an idle hope for a better life – and it is precisely by finally giving up this hope, Hegel argues, that the modern world can achieve, in its very rejection of a world beyond this one, the realization of the true Christian faith: a God come down to earth, a reconciliation of the human with the divine. Just because there is, in modernity, no longer any hope for a divine realm separate from the human, Hegel argues, modernity is precisely the place where the human and the divine can be reconciled, and the place where Christianity can finally be realized. This claim, perhaps the most paradoxical of all Hegel's beliefs, obviously demands more clarification.

One way to start is to look at what seems to be the opposite of this conception of Christian faith, the distinctly modern notion of enlightenment. In itself, the Enlightenment means the promotion of reason over religious dogmatism; the enlightened person is one who rejects appeals to faith and the supernatural and who asks for argument and evidence. In early modernity, appeal to argument and evidence meant appeal to the senses: religious claims were pushed aside in favor of natural science (most often understood in an empiricist way, as in Locke) and secular liberal politics (understood as promoting certain material ends, again as in Locke). But this kind of view depends on seeing sensations and desires as foundational for theoretical and practical claims, and as we have seen in Chapters 6 and 7, Hegel thinks that these kinds of foundational accounts turn out to fail. The history of enlightenment in the West, then, is such that the materialist claims used by the defenders of enlightenment to support their modern science and their modern politics turned out to be as dogmatic as the religious claims that were supposedly being left behind.

Excursus 3: Enlightenment

In one sense, the Enlightenment is a purely negative movement: it is the struggle of reason and truth against dogmatic appeals to supernatural authority. The Enlightenment seeks to combat the "tissue of superstitions, prejudices and errors" that has been foisted on the "mass of people" by the "deception" of priests and despots, an alliance "which, in its envious conceit, holds itself to be the sole possessor of insight and pursues its other selfish ends as well" (542). At the same time, the evil intentions of priests and despots cannot be the real object of enlightenment, which is supposed to be the publicly verifiable truth. Confronted with the demand for reason and evidence, the deceptions of dogmatists should simply melt away in the pure sunlight of truth. In this sense, it is puzzling that the defenders of enlightenment should trouble themselves with the claims of the faithful, since these are taken to be unreal and empty. To the extent that the Enlightenment is occupied with the struggle against dogmatism and superstition, then, it is because this struggle promises something more than the simple contemplation of the truth. The goal is the victory over "untruth and unreason" (547), the vanquishing of the superstition that the Enlightenment takes to have no reality at all. In its struggle with superstition, the Enlightenment occupies itself with unreal entities in order to satisfy itself (548). And this is exactly the Enlightenment's view of religious belief: "It is just this that Enlightenment rightly declares faith to be, when it says that what is for faith the absolute Being, is a Being of its own consciousness, is its own thought, something that is a creation of consciousness itself. Thus what Enlightenment declares to be an error and a fiction is the very same thing as Enlightenment itself is" (549).

At the same time, in trying to resist the pressures of the Enlightenment, faith equally ends up surrendering its own logic to that of its opponents, thus assuring its own defeat. According to the criticisms of enlightenment, religious believers put their trust in idols; they take material things as evidence of supernatural power, in order to satisfy their own longings for a better world. In one sense, the criticism is entirely unfair, because the object of religion is God, not any physical object: "What faith reveres, it certainly does not regard as stone or wood or dough, nor any kind of temporal, sensuous thing . . . faith does not regard such things as stones, etc. as possessing intrinsic being; on the contrary, what has intrinsic being for faith is solely the essential being of pure thought" (553). But if this is so, then there is also a sense in which the Enlightenment's critique of religion is entirely accurate. The source of faith is in fact the believer's own consciousness, and the believer's own needs. "Enlightenment that wants to teach faith the new wisdom does not tell it anything new; for its object is also for it just this, viz. a pure essence of its own consciousness, so that this consciousness does not take itself to be lost and negated in that object, but rather puts its trust in it . . . Whomever I trust, his *certainty of himself* is for me the *certainty of myself*; I recognize in him my own being-for-self, know that he acknowledges it and that is for him purpose and essence. Trust, however, is faith, because the consciousness of the believer is *directly related* to its object and is thus intuitively aware that it is *one* with it and in it" (549). But it is difficult for faith to admit this, because the believer takes himself to worship something more than himself and the objects of his own consciousness. To the extent that faith attempts to show that this is so, however, it can only end up contradicting itself, by trying to provide evidence of the objective existence of a God, evidence that enlightened thinkers can easily dismiss as unscientific and entirely false. "If faith wants to appeal to historical evidences in order to get that kind of foundation, or at least confirmation, of its content that Enlightenment talks about, and seriously thinks and acts as if that were a matter of importance, then it has already let itself be corrupted by the Enlightenment" (554).

What the secularism and materialism of the Enlightenment do, then, is to isolate and confine religious belief in the private realm of individual conviction and hope. They deprive religion of any objective content by subjecting it to a standard of scientific verification that faith can never meet.

As a result, faith has lost the content which filled its element, and collapses into a state in which it moves listlessly to and fro within itself. It has been expelled from its kingdom; or, this kingdom has been ransacked, since the waking consciousness has monopolized every distinction and expansion of it and has vindicated earth's ownership of every portion of it and given them back to earth. Yet faith is not on that account satisfied, for this illumination has everywhere brought to light only single, separate entities, so that what speaks to Spirit is only a reality without any substance, and a finitude forsaken by Spirit. Since faith is without content and cannot remain in this void, it is a *sheer yearning*, its truth an empty beyond, for which a fitting content can no longer be found, for everything is bestowed elsewhere. (573)

This description of religious faith should hardly seem new, because it is basically no different from Hegel's earlier description of the Unhappy Consciousness, which longs for a spiritual connection to the infinite while remaining chained to the finitude of this life. Has nothing changed from the ancient spiritual longings of the earliest Christians to the predicament of modern European Christians confronted with the secularism and materialism of the Enlightenment? In fact Hegel can admit that a great deal has changed, because as we have already noted, his position is not that ancient and modern Christian belief and practice are the same, but rather that modern historical conditions have led us to understand what was historically distinctive about ancient Christianity in a particular way. It is only through the secular pressures of the Enlightenment that we come to understand

Christianity as purely an attempt to resolve the tensions of the Unhappy Consciousness.

Of course, from the perspective of the Enlightenment, the Christian solution seems entirely lacking in rational justification. Therefore, it would seem to follow that the spiritual longings of faith should be left to the side, and that enlightened modern Europeans should content themselves with the material truths and satisfactions available to them in this life. But we have already seen that Hegel thinks that the Enlightenment itself sought more than this: in deriving satisfaction from its victories over superstition, the Enlightenment suggests a desire for something more than material truth. Even after religion has been pushed to the side, the Enlightenment's own commitment to materialism suggests a desire for an ultimate standard of truth that goes beyond anything that our senses can provide. Here Hegel reminds us of his arguments against empiricist conceptions of theoretical justification, the arguments we examined in Chapter 6. "In this connection, it is important to bear in mind that *pure matter* is merely what is *left over* when we *abstract* from seeing, feeling, tasting, etc., i.e. it is not matter that is seen, tasted, felt, etc., what is seen, felt, tasted, is not matter, but color, a stone, a salt, etc. Matter is rather a *pure abstraction*; and so what we are presented with here is the *pure essence of thought*, or pure thought as the Absolute" (577). In this passage, the failure of what we called in Chapter 6 the pure theoretical conception of knowledge is described as having its origins in exactly the source of religious faith: in our own desire to escape the finitude and imperfections of this world for a connection to an ultimate reality.

Once this specifically human desire is acknowledged for what it is, once it is cut off from any religious or putatively scientific connection to ultimate reality, we are left with no ultimate standards outside our own as human agents. And the consequence of this way of looking at the world is the claim that human agency itself is the source of ultimate value. "Spirit thus comes before us as *absolute freedom*. It is self-consciousness which grasps the fact that its certainty of itself is the essence of all the spiritual 'masses,' or spheres, of the real as well as of the supersensible world, or conversely, that essence and actuality are consciousness' knowledge of *itself*. It is conscious of its pure personality and therein of all spiritual reality, and all reality is solely spiritual; the world is for it simply its own will, and this is a general will" (584). Hegel's last reference is not just to Rousseau but also to the French revolutionary politics that he inspired. Those politics complete the Enlightenment's victory over its religious and aristocratic opponents, but for Hegel, the Revolution's victories did not and could not lead to any sort of stable political regime. Reprising his claim – familiar to us from our discussion of Stoicism and skepticism in Chapter 7 – that the notion of freedom, on its own, cannot provide any content for standards of conduct, Hegel argues that the spiritual longings that were always the hidden core of the Enlightenment now have nowhere to go, and can only turn on themselves. "Universal freedom, therefore, can produce neither a positive work nor a deed; there is left for it only *negative* action; it is merely the *fury* of destruction" (589). Freed from external constraints, the idea of human freedom can only act arbitrarily; its deeds are nothing but self-assertion, a self-assertion that reduces everything outside itself to meaninglessness:

The sole work and deed of universal freedom is therefore *death*, a death too which has no inner significance or filling, for what is negated is the empty point of the absolutely free self. It is thus the coldest and meanest of all deaths, with no more significance than cutting off a head of cabbage or swallowing a mouthful of water. (590)

. . . it is absolutely impossible for it [the post-revolutionary government] to exhibit itself as anything else but a *faction*. What is called government is merely the *victorious* faction, and in the very fact of its being a faction lies the direct necessity of its overthrow; and its being government makes it, conversely, into a faction, and guilty. When the universal will maintains that what the government has actually done is a crime committed against it, the government, for its part, has nothing specific and outwardly apparent by which the guilt of the will opposed to it could be demonstrated; for what stands opposed to it as the *actual* universal will is only an unreal pure will, *intention. Being suspected,* therefore, takes the place, or has the significance and effect, of *being guilty;* and the external reaction against this reality that lies in the simple inwardness of intention, consists in the cold, matter-of-fact annihilation of this existent self, from which nothing else can be taken away but its mere being. (591)

In these justly famous passages, the Reign of Terror is understood not as a corruption of the original revolutionary principle of liberty (a characteristic feature of liberal interpretations of the French Revolution), nor as a proof that the revolutionaries were never really committed to liberty at all (a characteristic feature of conservative interpretations). Instead, Hegel understands the violence of the Terror as the consequence of the principle of liberty itself. The notion of human freedom is really the ancient ethical and spiritual longing for a better world, which, in the wake of the Enlightenment and the Revolution, is finally cut off from any connection to a reality beyond the longing itself. Deprived of any opportunity to express itself objectively, the free will becomes nothing but pure subjectivity, asserting itself in arbitrary acts of destruction. The heirs of the Enlightenment do everything they accused their religious opponents of doing, and far worse.

One way of looking at these developments would be to say, as many contemporary postmodernists do, that both Christianity and modernity have been discredited, and discredited in the same way. Hegel's reaction is quite different. He fully welcomes the conclusion that the Enlightenment's demand for rational justification is nothing more than a version of earlier religious longing. Hegel wants to isolate – or, better, to claim that the events of modernity have isolated – the pure longing for universal justification from the specifics of any particular claim to justification, which, in its specificity, will necessarily fall short of the hope of full justification. And in recognizing this distinction – and accepting it as inevitable – we can become reconciled to it in a way that earlier cultures could not. Since modernity has led us to recognize the demand for justification as merely a religious hope that cannot be fully realized, it is possible for modern culture to appreciate the value of this hope in a way that earlier cultures, who truly sought its realization, could not. On Hegel's view, after the fragmentation of Greek culture, after the collapse of medieval religious dogmatism and the failure of early modernity to legitimate itself, we can now, finally, understand the idea of justification as not a state of affairs that could be realized, but as a demand that human beings bring to the world – a demand that has shaped the history of our culture but that no culture could ever fully realize. But in accepting this point, we accept the notion of a culture, a distinctly modern culture, which was not disappointed that it failed to satisfy this demand. Such a culture would not be devastated – as on Hegel's account, the Greek world was – that it failed to fully satisfy the demand for justification. Rather such a culture would accept the demand for justification as a shaping force in its history, as a productive source of cultural ferment and change, and in so doing, would become reconciled to this demand as a valuable even though unsatisfiable hope. In this kind of reconciliation, the longing expressed in the Christian faith could finally find a place in the world. And it is this that explains Hegel's most paradoxical claim: that the very difficulty of Christian faith under conditions of modern secularism not only allows us to understand better the nature of that faith, but also allows us to realize that faith for the first time.

Excursus 4: Morality

The first lesson of Hegel's account of modernity is that we finally come to learn why our demands for justification cannot be satisfied: because the demand for justification comes from ourselves as subjects, not from anything about the objects of the world. But the second lesson of Hegel's account is that we learn the first lesson only through a painful historical experience, which teaches us that the sharp separation between the subject's demands for justification and the objects which fail to live up to them is itself a recipe for disappointment. The distinction has a kind of validity in the nature of thought, in the consciousness of an individual subject. But that validity evaporates in the actions and lives of individuals, who must commit themselves to particular courses of action, to specific standards of value that are tainted with contingency and finitude. In that sense, the pure rational demands of subjects do not finally serve our true interests as subjects. We must therefore find another way to accommodate this aspect of ourselves.

For Hegel, the best illustration of these lessons is provided by Kant's moral philosophy, because its central claim is that morality has no objective existence outside of the self-legislation of rational agents. To be moral, for Kant, is to conform to an objective law of duty, a source of unconditional obligation. But if the agent's conformity to this law is to be good without qualification, then its goodness cannot depend on anything outside conformity to the law itself – for instance, on a purpose that the law of duty might be intended to serve. In that case, the intended purpose, and not the law itself, would be the candidate for unconditional goodness. So Kant concludes that moral goodness is found simply in an agent's conforming to law, in the agent's commitment to actions that could have the form of universality. These actions are not objectively good in the sense that their goodness could be observed or verified; the results of an action are not what determine the morality of an action. What matters is the agent's own internal commitment to universal law. Morality is about having the right sort of motive, the motive of duty, but conformity to duty is at the same time the autonomous willing of a rational agent, the agent's judgment that his or her actions are justified because they are candidates for universal rules of conduct.

As his metaphor of the kingdom of ends is meant to suggest, Kant's autonomous moral agent is a kind of legislator, prescribing principles of action for potential commonwealths of rational beings. The autonomous agent seeks to impose this legislation on the world, and this task of imposition raises the question of whether the imposition can succeed. Is our world one in which moral action is possible and effective? On the one hand, the Kantian moral agent is supposed to be indifferent to the workings of nature. Moral legislation is self-legislation, the free act of an agent who is not bound to any standards of conduct that are not of the agent's own making, and the moral agent ought to conform to those standards no matter what the circumstances of the world happen to be. On the other hand, the moral agent is still a natural creature, and must act within the confines of the empirical world. The moral agent's duty is to transform the empirical world along moral lines, and in that sense, the moral agent cannot be indifferent to what happens in the world (599–601).

Kant's account of the relation between morality and happiness is an especially instructive example of this tension. On the one hand, morality has nothing to do with happiness: we should do our duty whether or not it happens to make us happy. Whether we are happy and whether we are good are two very different questions, and the fact that the virtuous sometimes suffer while the wicked flourish can even help us to appreciate the value of an independent or pure morality. On the other hand, we all do desire happiness, and so as empirically situated moral agents, we cannot help regretting the sufferings of the virtuous and the flourishing of the vicious. Moral action should make the world a better place, which would mean bringing morality and happiness into proper alignment. But this is not something humans can do: only an all-powerful, all-knowing, and completely good God could see to it that the wicked are punished while the virtuous are rewarded. So Kant adds to his moral theory the "practical postulate" of God's existence; that is, he argues that a moral agent must believe in a God who will dispense justice after death. Without this belief, he argues, we would have to see moral action as amounting to nothing. Still, it is hard to see how the postulate of God finally helps us with the project of moral action, because if there is divine justice in the afterlife, then human beings are not doing anything in this world to bring about that justice. It looks like all we can do on earth is to fulfill our duty, and so the human project of transforming our world into a moral one amounts to nothing. But it was that project that supposedly prompted our belief in God in the first place.

On Hegel's view, the Kantian moral consciousness is always "dissembling"; it cannot be honest with itself about whether it cares about the indifference of the empirical world to the purposes of morality. The moral consciousness defines itself through this indifference, but at the same time, it cannot conceive of itself as actually accomplishing anything in the world without at the same time renouncing that indifference. Even if we forget the larger question of the distribution of happiness and focus only on the dutiful actions of each agent, the problem recurs. We are all supposed to act morally, but does this in fact occur? What the world shows us are the results of our actions, not the pure motives and unconditional principles that could provide our behavior with moral justification. As Kant himself says, we cannot be sure that there has ever been a case of true moral action in the entire history of humanity. Do we care about this? On the one hand, it should not matter; we know what duty requires of us, and we ought to carry it out no matter what anyone else is doing or has ever done. So we act, but even our own deeds cannot show the purity of motive that is the defining feature of moral action. In that sense, the world is always a disappointment to us; the actions of everyone appear to us as potentially driven by hidden motives, and thus as examples of hypocrisy and evil. No moral action can ever match the purity of the thought of the moral consciousness itself. But since it is the moral consciousness' purpose to act, it can never be satisfied with itself.

It lacks the power to externalize itself, the power to make itself into a Thing, and to endure being. It lives in dread of besmirching the splendor of its inner being by action and an existence, and, in order to preserve the purity of its heart, it flees from contact with the actual world, and persists in its self-willed impotence to renounce its self which is reduced to the extreme of ultimate abstraction . . . The hollow thought which it has produced for itself now fills it, therefore, with a sense of emptiness. Its activity is a yearning which merely loses itself as consciousness becomes an object devoid of substance, and rising above this loss, and falling back on itself, finds itself only as a lost soul. In this transparent purity of its moments, an unhappy, so called "beautiful soul," its light dies away within it, and it vanishes like a shapeless vapor that dissolves into thin air. (658)

We have seen this kind of impasse many times thus far – in our discussions of the Unhappy Consciousness, the solitary ethical individual in ancient Greece, and the difficulty of religious faith during the Enlightenment. In all of these cases, the world seems inadequate to what Hegel calls the power and the infinitude of thought, to our spiritual and rational demands. There is an intentional repetitiveness to Hegel's historical narrative, because he wants to argue that a certain inheritance from ancient Greek and Christian thinking is still at work in the modern world. On the other hand, it is only in the modern world that we can come to understand this inheritance in the proper way. The impasse of the Kantian moral agent, of Hegel's "beautiful soul," is in one crucial way different from its historical antecedents: its self-consciousness. The Kantian moral agent is conscious that the world is inadequate to its demands precisely because its demands are entirely its own. That is what Kantian moral autonomy means.

For that reason, when "beautiful soul" recognizes its impasse, it cannot finally blame the world. Rather it must blame itself for creating the impasse.

And it must therefore forgive the world – and all the acting agents in the world – for its seeming imperfections. For those imperfections are imperfections only from the perspective of the demands of thought. At the same time, those demands are not themselves any sort of indictment of thought itself, which (for Kant and Hegel alike) really is the source of power and infinity. In that sense, what the formerly dissembling Kantian moral consciousness must forgive is not finally the world, but rather itself for demanding that the world conform to its demands – and for blaming itself in the process. For the Kantian moral consciousness, the actions of others appeared only as examples of potential hypocrisy. Now we can recognize that this appearance was itself the product of the Kantian moral consciousness' own demands, and we can allow that the actions of others can themselves be the product of a similar consciousness. Regarding the actions of others (or even of oneself) in this way requires a surrender of the claim that the world is inadequate to the demands of thought or, more specifically, of the claim that the appearances of the world cannot manifest those demands. In forgiving others, we recognize them as consciousnesses like ourselves, who are equally trying to realize the infinite demands of consciousness within the finitude of the world.

The forgiveness which it extends to the other is the renunciation of itself, of its *unreal* essential being which it put on a level with that other which was a *real* action, and acknowledges that what thought characterized as bad, viz. action, is good; or rather it abandons this distinction of the specific thought and its *subjectively* determined judgment, just as the other abandons its *subjective* characterization of action. The word of reconciliation is the *objectively* existent Spirit, which beholds the pure knowledge of itself *qua universal* essence, in its opposite, in the pure knowledge of itself *qua* absolutely self-contained and exclusive *individuality* – a reciprocal recognition which is *absolute* Spirit. (670)

This moment of reconciliation is the culmination of the entire *Phenomenology*. The infinitely longing consciousness drops its opposition to the world, and thereby loses its dissatisfaction with itself:

Through this externalization, this knowledge which in its existence is self-discordant returns into the unity of the *self*. It is the *actual* "I," the universal knowledge of itself in its absolute opposite, in the knowledge which remains *internal*, and which, on account of the purity of its separate *being-within-self*, is completely universal. The reconciling *Yea,* in which the two "I"s let go their antithetical *existence,* is the *existence* of the "I" which has expanded into a duality, and therein remains identical with itself, and its complete externalization and opposite, possesses the certainty of itself: it is God manifested in the midst of those who know themselves in the form of pure knowledge. (671)

What Hegel's idea of reconciliation means is that in the modern world, we are able to recognize the failures of our ultimate ethical, spiritual, and rational demands as the natural result of the collision between thought and the world. And having understood the source of these failures, we need no longer conclude that the world cannot reflect the reality of thought. Instead we can see the history of culture, the passage from the ancient to the modern world, as itself the work of thought's demands. In that sense, the finite world is full of the expression of the infinite power of thought, just as Christianity promised (but could never rationally explain).

Telling this kind of story finally requires an argument that modern culture does in fact provide us with frameworks and institutions that are reconciled to the demand for justification in the way I have just described, as a productive force that is to be valued even if the demand can never finally be met. In the end, the *Phenomenology*'s account of morality and forgiveness, of modernity's reconciliation to the finitude of the world, only gestures toward such an argument. In Hegel's work, one might do better to look at the argument of the *Philosophy of Right,* in which he defends the view that the modern state is an institution of just this sort.[9] But we can at least sketch the kind of argument Hegel needs here. Drastically summarized, the claim will be that the main institutions of modern culture – natural science and liberal democratic politics – are characterized by a kind of inclusiveness and fallibilism that allow for competing claims of justification from parties of all sorts, yet are not destroyed by the plurality of such claims or by their failure to gain full acceptance. The idea here is that these institutions accept – in a way that earlier, pre-modern cultures did not – the provisional and constructed nature of theories and political identities, so that the overturnings of particular theoretical or practical claims discredit neither the institutions of natural science or of liberal democratic politics nor the ongoing attempts at justification that take place within them. Of course there is no guarantee that we will see failures of justification in this way. We might well despair of the ability of our particular cultural institutions to cope with the multiplicity and transience of claims to justification, and despair of our own abilities to continue to press claims to justification under such conditions. But Hegel's larger claim is that, looking back over the history of attempts at justification, we have good reason not to retreat to despair. Doing so will inevitably resurrect an opposition between the

---

[9] In arguing that the account of the *Philosophy of Right* is needed to complete the argument set out in the *Phenomenology,* I am in agreement with the reading proposed by Pinkard, *Hegel's Phenomenology,* pp. 261–274.

hope for full justification and the actual cultural institutions which always fall short of that hope, and this kind of opposition can only lead to the sort of disappointments that befell the Greek, the medieval Christian, and even the early modern world. Hegel's larger claim is that only the later modern world, after experiencing these disappointments, has succeeded in constructing a cultural framework that can contain this kind of opposition and that can reconcile us to it. In that sense, the argument is that even large-scale modern cultural breakdowns (the First World War, the rise of totalitarianism) cannot finally discredit the modern idea of a pluralistic, fallibilist cultural framework where competing claims to justification can be welcomed without loss to the larger framework itself.

REVIEW OF THE ARGUMENT

This chapter has been sufficiently long and complex that we will benefit here from a synoptic account of its argument, one that connects these historical themes back to our earlier discussions of culture. We began by noting that Hegel's negative arguments against the pure notions of the theoretical and then the practical self seem to leave us with the conclusion that claims to knowledge and to value cannot be vindicated in any sort of general way, that such vindication can only happen within particular historical contexts. This looks like a kind of weak form of communitarianism or even cultural relativism, but Hegel wants to make much stronger claims for his position, and we needed to understand how he could do that. And so we argued that the historical sections of the *Phenomenology* are included not simply to fill in the particular details of "our" cultural contexts, but more importantly to deal with the philosophical problem raised by the relativization of justification to cultural contexts. How can we be sure that our claims to justification are not dangerously distorted by the culture we have inherited? How can we affirm our commitment to the validity of any norms if that commitment is itself shaped by a socialization process that is not under our rational control? How can we affirm culture and normativity if they are, in one sense, just the effects of potentially arbitrary socialization? How can we reconcile ourselves to this fact and still affirm some meaningful account of rational justification?

Hegel's answer is that we can do this if we reflect on the history of Western culture, and particularly on the way this history has been characterized and even driven by an ongoing tension between the fact of cultural norms and the demand for rational justification. Looking back from the perspective of modernity, Hegel wants us to understand this demand as a kind of free-floating force (which he often calls "pure negativity") through which each individual reveals his or her freedom, the power and right to interrogate all existing norms. This force was introduced into Western culture by dissenting individuals like Antigone, Socrates, and Jesus, who challenged existing cultural norms in terms of a deeper ethical good. But the attempt to realize this kind of absolute moral demand, this demand for full justification, in an actual set of norms proved unsuccessful, both in Greek philosophical formalist and in Christian, otherworldly terms. That led to the modern reaction against religious ideals, but this reaction implied a foundational materialism that was ultimately as dogmatic and as unsatisfiable as the religious claims it hoped to displace. Retrospectively, Hegel argues, we should see this entire history as teaching us to distinguish between the demand for justification and the idea of a fully justified set of norms; the first is a real and productive human desire, and the second is an abstract and ultimately unattainable goal. Linking them together, believing that the first must imply a commitment to the second, can only produce a kind of dissatisfaction with the world as failing to live up to our expectations. Hegel's view is that in the modern world, we are finally able to move beyond this sort of dissatisfaction through cultural and institutional frameworks that honor the demand for justification while accepting that full justification can never be achieved. In one sense, the philosophical problem raised by the problem of culture is dissolved, because we abandon the hope that our present cultural norms, or any other set of norms, could ever be ultimately justified. But in another sense, that problem is solved, because the sort of cultural norms that accept that point, the sort of norms that Hegel thinks govern modern institutions, are precisely the norms that are justified.

CHAPTER 9

Results

If the reading given in the previous four chapters is right, we can say that Hegel takes himself to have established two main claims. First, he takes himself to have shown, negatively, that no general account of theoretical or practical reason is possible. Such an account would begin, in the theoretical case, with the bare idea of an objective account of the world, freed of any contribution by us as inquiring agents or, in the practical case, from the bare idea of an agent pursuing something that the agent claims to be of value, freed of any constraint imposed by the world. In similar fashion, Hegel argues that these bare conceptions will fall short of anything we would recognize as a determinate claim of knowledge or of value. Anything we would recognize as a justified theoretical or practical claim, Hegel takes himself to have shown, must take place within an existing context of norms of belief and of action. Reasoning, then, is culturally and historically constrained.

Second, Hegel takes himself to have shown that the fact of cultural constraint implies a philosophical problem about how anything can be justified at all. Here Hegel argues that the problem can neither be solved directly nor simply dismissed, because it arises from the collision of two irreducible features of our lives: first, our nature as free and rational beings who have the power and right to question any norm; and second, our nature as cultural and historical beings who think and act within a context of norms that have been imposed upon us. We can see this by reflecting back on the history of Western culture, and seeing that history as the free and rational subject's struggle against the fact of cultural constraint, a struggle that could never finally be successful. In retrospect, we are able to understand the idea of fully justified norms not as an achievable state of affairs, but as an expression of our free and rational nature that we have tried, unsuccessfully, to impose on the world; this is the lesson Hegel thinks we can learn from his narrative that takes us from Socrates to the development of Christianity and then through the Enlightenment. Understanding this history leads us to see that these two features of our nature cannot be eliminated, but rather must be reconciled. And Hegel thinks they can be reconciled in the modern world, because the modern world has gone through the history of trying to solve or dismiss the problem and now can accept its insolubility. That means that the modern norms that do reconcile them are justified in a way that earlier norms are not; hence it is false to say that the fact of cultural constraint means that nothing can be justified.

What we now need to understand is how this positive conclusion is supposed to follow from what I have just called Hegel's two main claims: the impossibility of pure theoretical and pure practical reason, and then the stubbornness of the problem of culture. These main claims are essentially negative, even skeptical, and yet Hegel wants to draw from them a strongly positive conclusion: that the norms of the modern West are fully justified. By "fully justified," Hegel intends more than a weak historicist or communitarian claim, that the norms are justified merely "to us" – that is, to those of us who occupy a certain historical and/or cultural location. Though he understands the history of the norms of modernity as essential to their justification, Hegel also regards those norms as rationally superior to those of other actual and possible cultures. Though Hegel's method of argument is intended to break with the conceptions of justification proposed in the philosophical tradition from Plato through Descartes to Kant, his aspiration to justification is exactly the same. His claim is that the norms of the modern West are valid, in some incontrovertible sense. We have already noted that this conclusion is underdetermined by the argument of the *Phenomenology*, since Hegel's defense of the norms of the modern West is not complete without the description of those norms laid out most fully in the *Philosophy of Right*. But though the *Phenomenology* is not a full defense of the norms of the modern West, it is a defense of a certain kind of argument for them, and that argument is supposed to satisfy a deep philosophical desire for full justification. In fact Hegel believes that his position is the one the philosophical tradition has been searching for all along. But it is only now, looking backward, that we are able to understand this. And that point itself suggests how Hegel can move from his negative or skeptical arguments to his positive and sweeping conclusion, from his emphasis on culture and history to a trans-cultural and trans-historical claim. The answer, stated as briefly as possible, is the idea of retrospective self-knowledge.

RETROSPECTION AND JUSTIFICATION

Here is a simple psychological point that everyone understands: it is possible for a negative experience to yield a positive lesson. More specifically, it is possible to try to achieve a goal, and fail, and yet regard this failure as ultimately productive, if the failure allows us to see, for the first time, that the goal is not one that we really do or should have in the first place. In this kind of retrospective narrative, the negative experience yields positive self-knowledge.

Hegel wants us to understand his negative arguments in just this way. The failure to articulate a purely theoretical and then a purely practical standpoint is what leads us to the problem of cultural constraint. And the history of failure of attempts to solve the problem of cultural constraint directly is what leads us to a modern self-consciousness about the limits of full rational justification, a sense that the problem of culture should be dissolved in a different way. It is that self-consciousness, and its expression in modern cultural norms, that constitutes the positive content of Hegel's skeptical arguments.

But it is important to see that the positive outcome here is not just any lesson, but a lesson about the inevitability of this sort of retrospective narrative in general. The failures that Hegel describes in his skeptical arguments are precisely the failures of schemes of justification that deny the importance of our historicity. Such schemes of justification try to articulate conceptions of the world that make no reference, first, to us as subjects; second, to us as subjects not constrained by cultural norms; and third, to us as subjects trying to flee this cultural constraint. The *Phenomenology* is essentially a retelling of the history of Western philosophy and culture, now described as a series of failures of justification. What we are supposed to gain from these negative experiences is a positive acceptance of ourselves as the sort of beings who are who we are because we have inherited certain cultural norms, and who have worked to gain a sense of ourselves as free and rational agents by struggling with our relation to these cultural norms. That, Hegel wants to say, is what human beings essentially are, and in this sense his positive argument is an argument for a certain conception of subjectivity. But since this conception of subjectivity sees human beings as essentially engaged in a struggle for self-understanding with and against their cultural norms, the conception of subjectivity also implies a view about what would satisfy us as subjects: a conception of ourselves that would ease this struggle, and reconcile us to the fact of cultural constraint. And we have already seen that Hegel thinks that it is only in retrospect, in looking back at the struggle and learning to give it up, that we both escape from the struggle and learn who we are.

So the positive lesson that emerges from looking back over the history of attempts at justification without retrospective narration is that retrospective narration is essential to who we are as human beings. And that allows Hegel to turn his negative or skeptical arguments about justification into two positive claims:

(1) It is an essential feature of human beings that they are beings who can and must understand themselves retrospectively by telling a historical story about how they came to be what they are.
(2) It is only in the modern world, after passing through and retrospectively understanding the historical experience of Western culture, that we can understand and convincingly articulate thesis (1).

Notice the way these theses are mutually reinforcing: (1) says we are beings who need historical stories, and (2) is a historical story that gets us to (1). The account of human subjectivity in (1) is historical and is justified historically in (2), and what makes the narrative in (2) justifying (rather than just a historical story) is that it both defends and follows the account of subjectivity in (1). There is a kind of circularity here, but Hegel denies that it is vicious; in fact his claim is exactly the opposite. His view is that the idea of retrospective subjectivity can justify itself, through a retrospectively subjective narrative, and therefore does not depend on an appeal to an external justification (which would itself have to be defended). A very old problem in philosophy, which goes back to the ancient skeptics, wonders how justification is possible at all, because any justification would itself have to be justified in terms of something else, and so on *ad infinitum*. Hegel's response to this problem is that his defense of retrospective subjectivity is not an appeal to something beyond retrospective subjectivity, but simply an example of retrospective subjects trying to understand themselves retrospectively. How can an example of retrospective self-understanding also count as a justification of retrospective self-understanding? The answer is that what we come to retrospectively understand in this example is that attempts at justification that ignore retrospective self-understanding are doomed to failure.

Still there seems to be a problem here. It is one thing to argue, negatively, that attempts at justification that ignore our cultural and historical nature, that seek to defend theoretical and practical norms without regard to an existing context of norms, are doomed to failure. And it is another thing to argue that human beings always seek to understand themselves by looking back at how they came to be who they are today, by reflecting on their histories. But is there really a deep connection between these claims? Both make an essential reference to cultural and historical context, but the first claim is essentially about justification, while the second claim is essentially about self-understanding. The first claim says that justifications will always be culturally and historically constrained, while the second claim says that self-understanding will be constrained in a similar way. But the fact of cultural constraint does not yet suggest a deep connection between the notions of justification and retrospective self-understanding, and without that connection, Hegel's positive conclusions do not follow. As we have already seen, Hegel's defense of the norms of the modern West is essentially that these norms reflect the history of earlier, failed attempts at justification. Thus these norms reflect a deeper self-understanding, and they are justified for exactly this reason. But that argument presumes a connection between justification and self-understanding; indeed, Hegel's position seems to be just that retrospective self-understanding *is* justification, and vice versa. What is supposed to justify Hegel's account of modernity is that it provides us with a certain self-understanding. But why should this self-understanding count as justification? So far the only connection between self-understanding and justification seems to be the notion of cultural and historical constraint, but why should this guarantee an essential rather than an accidental connection between self-understanding and justification?

Hegel's answer here is that the notion of self-understanding does imply an essential connection to justification, because his notion of retrospective self-understanding itself emerged from a struggle with attempts at justification, and because the self-understanding that emerged from this struggle itself includes a recognition of our deep desire for justification. It is true that Hegel's second claim concerns only our need to understand ourselves within our cultural and historical context, but an essential part of what we are trying to understand about ourselves is our desire to justify cultural norms, and how we can reconcile this desire with the fact of cultural constraint. As we saw in Chapter 8, what the modern self-understanding is supposed to understand is precisely that our desire for justification can never be fully satisfied, but still serves as a productive motor for historical and cultural change. So Hegel's argument for modernity is not just that it achieves a certain self-understanding, but also that this self-understanding is able to find a place for the demand for justification that earlier cultural understandings could not. Looking back over the failed history of attempts at justification, we find that the modern world is reconciled to the inevitability and the unsatisfiability of the demand for justification in a way earlier cultures were not.

The connection between self-understanding and justification, then, is supposed to be this: that we achieve self-understanding precisely by reflecting on the things we took to be justifying, and we end our struggle for justification precisely by coming to a self-understanding that reconciles us to our failures at justification, by showing them to be productive of the people we now understand ourselves to be. The demand for full or unconditional justification, the traditional desire of the philosopher, is thus shown to be an essential "moment" of self-understanding. We understand ourselves by looking at the history of our attempts at justification, and by seeing them as necessary for making us who we are, we satisfy both our demand for justification and our need to understand ourselves. Self-understanding and justification may seem to be two different things, but in a successful retrospective narrative of our attempts at justification, they are reconciled to one another. For Hegel, retrospective self-understanding is justification, because only retrospective self-understanding can satisfy our urge for justification, by placing it in a narrative where it can reach an end, the notion of retrospective self-understanding itself.

HEGEL IN THE HISTORY OF PHILOSOPHY: A REVIEW

Hegel's standing in the history of philosophy rests finally on the claim just sketched, that his account of retrospective self-understanding satisfies, for the first time, the philosophical demand for justification. And since an essential argument for this claim is Hegel's claim that the history of philosophy consists of failed attempts to meet this demand, we can evaluate Hegel's claim only by thinking about the history of philosophy and seeing whether Hegel has been able to do something his predecessors could not. Or, more accurately, we need to think about the history of philosophy and see whether Hegel has been able to do something because his predecessors could not do what they were trying to do. Doing that will allow us a summary look at the thesis of this study: that Hegel's project is to defend a certain conception of subjectivity, of subjectivity as retrospective self-understanding, and that this conception of subjectivity can be given a new, historical, but still fully rational justification.

Western philosophy begins with a demand for justification, issued by Socrates to his interlocutors. As Plato understood Socrates, that demand can be satisfied only through knowledge of a special kind of object, a Form, whose nature was both fully explanatory (things are the way they are because of their participation in Forms) and fully justifying (the Forms are objects not just of knowledge but also of goodness, since studying them is the highest activity for human beings). Even those Greek philosophers who differed with the Platonic notion of a Form still retained Plato's view that philosophy was a demand for knowledge of a special kind of object, whose rational contemplation constituted the best form of human life.

With Descartes, modern philosophy replaced the substantive demand for knowledge of a special, purely rational object with the procedural demand for a proper method to know ordinary, material objects. But it was only in Kant that this methodological turn was fully theorized and finally given full expression. Cartesian rationalism and Lockean empiricism ultimately remain forms of Platonism, because their methodologies rely on foundational appeals to certain privileged ideas (intellectual ideas in the case of rationalism, simple sense-impressions in the case of empiricism) that themselves become the special objects of theoretical knowledge. Unlike the *Meditations*, however, the *Critique of Pure Reason* is not a search for knowledge, but rather an investigation of how empirical knowledge is possible, and Kant's answer is famously that our minds provide a special sort of framework (spatio-temporal, causally structured) that makes objective assertions possible. But though the pure forms of intuition and the categories may appear to be foundational ideas, they dictate nothing about the content of knowledge. They say only what it would mean for something to count as knowledge, and their derivation is meant to be entirely procedural: something can count as knowledge if it can be verified in an experience that could be judged by all. Knowledge that can be had and communicated by everyone, not knowledge of any special kind of object, becomes the guiding principle of Kant's theoretical philosophy.

We are then left with the question of what gives this principle of universal accessibility its privileged status, and there Kant's answer is that it is a form of the principle of universality that finds its full expression in the moral or practical realm. Or, more precisely, it is the same principle of universality, but it is only in the practical realm that it has a fully rational status. Kant's argument here is that a theoretical claim that has the form of universality, that appeals to an experience that could be judged by all, is only a candidate for rational knowledge, not rational knowledge in itself. There is no fully rational knowledge, for Kant, because all knowledge is empirical, and empirical knowledge is simply knowledge of what is, not why it had to be that way. So no knowledge will ever be self-justifying in the way Plato conceived knowledge of the Forms. But in the practical realm, Kant holds that a claim that has the form of universality, a claim that says that something is good for everyone to do that everyone could in fact do, is rationally justified in the way no theoretical claim ever is. That is, Kant believes that a person who acts out of duty, which he understands as acting for the reason that everyone could (or could not) do something, is acting with full justification. A morally committed agent, unlike a theoretical inquirer, can be fully rational.

On Kant's view, though, a moral agent is merely proposing a maxim that he or she thinks would be good for everyone to do. Since the agent is moral, the maxim meets a necessary condition for justification to all rational agents: it would be possible for everyone to act on the maxim, if they too thought it to be good. But this is far from any sufficient condition for justification: we cannot say that the maxim really is good for everyone to act on, only that they could act on it, if they accepted the agent's own judgment that the maxim was good to act on. In that sense, a universalizable maxim is only a candidate for goodness, not fully good in itself, just as an empirically grounded claim is only a candidate for knowledge, not knowledge in the fullest sense. In counting the agent's maxim as fully justified, Kant is allowing the agent's own judgment, which has only the bare form of rationality, to count as fully rational. And if asked why we should do this, Kant can say only that we owe it to the agent as an autonomous being who can will laws of his or her own, and whose autonomous choices are worthy of respect for just that reason (i.e., because they are autonomous). Thus we can say that Kant's categorical imperative is not a fully justified principle of practical reason, but rather a procedural substitute for such a principle, which we are to allow to count as a fully justified principle out of respect for the autonomy and dignity of each person.[1]

Read one way, this capsule history is a story of the failure of the philosophical search for justification in both its substantive, Platonic and its procedural, Kantian form. Read another way, however, the story is also a kind of etiology of the philosophical search for justification as ultimately a product of our own autonomy. As we sketched it previously, the Kantian, procedural conception of justification is less a discovery of a justified conception of reason than an attempt to promote the choices of human beings to a fully rational status. The search for rational justification turns out to be the expression of agents trying to legitimate their own activity. This diagnosis could be an embarrassment for the philosophical search for justification, if we understood this desire for legitimation as an illegitimate supplanting of rationality by self-promotion. But if we could understand this desire in a positive way, as somehow justified in itself, we could see the unmasking of philosophical justification as revealing of a deeper and in no sense embarrassing truth.

---

[1] I discuss these issues further in my "How Kantian Is Constructivism?" *Kant-Studien* 90:4 (1999), pp. 385–409, especially pp. 400–404.

Hegel's innovation, now for the last time, is to understand the human desire for (self-)legitimation as productive of theoretical and practical innovation and discovery, as a motor of historical change, including and especially the historical change that allowed us, in the modern world, to understand this point itself. If Platonic rationality is to be supplanted by Kantian autonomy, then Kantian autonomy will itself have to be legitimated, and Hegel's method is to legitimate it retrospectively, as crucial for making us who we have come to be, including and especially crucial for allowing us to see that we are beings who need to understand ourselves retrospectively. And because the history of the failure of substantive and procedural rationality is itself the justification of the claim that we are retrospective self-knowers, we can say that this failure, understood retrospectively, turns out, paradoxically, to satisfy the philosophical desire for justification, in a retrospective self-knowledge of ourselves as retrospective self-knowers.

A CRUCIAL AMBIGUITY

We have just said that Hegel wants to redescribe the Platonic quest for truth as the expression of Kantian autonomy, and then to legitimate Kantian autonomy by "placing" it as a crucial moment in a retrospective narrative that tells us who we are. How, though, does this satisfy the original Platonic urge? There is a crucial ambiguity here about who has this urge, and whether it really can be satisfied in the sense that anyone who actually has it would want.

On the one hand, it would seem that Hegel is saying that the desire for ultimate justification is the desire of earlier historical actors, or earlier versions of ourselves, who fail to satisfy it in the form they have it. Our retrospective self-knowledge then consists in seeing their, or our, earlier failures as productive of who we are today. But in this sort of story, we ourselves are beyond the desire for ultimate justification: we see it from the perspective of a wise but also chastened maturity, as people who have learned something from an earlier failure. So it looks like the desire for ultimate justification is never satisfied: our earlier selves try for it and fail, and we look at their failure and learn to give it up.

Hegel tries to avoid this conclusion by arguing that the lesson we learn itself satisfies the desire for ultimate justification. We now accept the limits of claims to justification, and the necessity of retrospective self-knowledge, in a way that our earlier selves did not, and this acceptance itself is fully justified. But in what sense does this acceptance satisfy the original desire? We can say, retrospectively, that it was a good thing that our earlier selves had the desire; this is what is implied in describing the search for full justification as the motor of historical change. But that claim will not work for our present and future selves, who have moved beyond the naïve desires of our youthful selves. In fact it is hard to see how the claim about the motor of historical change could continue to be true beyond the present, once we accept the lessons of our earlier failures of justification. Since the desire for full justification is not satisfied by our earlier or future selves in the role of historical actors, as inquirers or agents pressing the demand for full justification, Hegel is driven to say that it can only be satisfied by our present selves in the role of retrospective knowers, looking back at the adventures of our earlier selves. On this view, the desire for full justification is satisfied by the superiority of retrospective self-knowledge, the wisdom of the mature triumphing over the naïveté of youth.

It is true that any retrospective narrative automatically asserts its superiority to the earlier perspectives it works to analyze, by ultimately comprehending them as stages on the way to understanding who we are. This is the truth in the original idealist assumption that history – understood not as the unfolding of events but as the rational comprehension of events that have already unfolded – is always progressive, an assumption that has been fiercely attacked but can never finally be refuted. (The historians who insist on not judging the past by the "superior" standards of the present are thereby congratulating themselves for their superiority to earlier historians, which is exactly the sort of claim they are supposed to be refuting.) There is no way to tell a good retrospective narrative without assuming a knowing and therefore superior position over the actors described in the narrative, who, no matter how sophisticated and thoughtful they are, always occupy the position of the naïve. Their choices may be elaborately reasoned, but from the perspective of the retrospective narrative, they are always missing something, which is just the wider perspective that the retrospective narrative is trying to supply.[2]

But we should not confuse the superiority presumed in any retrospective narrative with the claim that retrospective narrative itself is always the superior or indeed the supreme form of inquiry. Certainly any particular retrospective narrative can be supplanted by a further retrospective narrative which places the earlier narration in the inferior or naïve position. So it never made any sense for anyone to criticize Hegel for trying to have the last word on any particular historical phenomenon. If he seemed like he

---

[2] For a very interesting discussion of these issues about the nature and logic of retrospective narrative, see Ermanno Bencivenga, *Hegel's Dialectical Logic* (Oxford University Press, 2000), especially chapter 5.

was having the last word, it was only because any retrospective narrative does this, and it always was and always will remain open for anyone else to supply an updated and better narrative.[3] What Hegel did try to say, though, was that retrospective narratives were superior to earlier, failed methods of philosophical inquiry, and that we had now come to realize this, at this point in the history of the modern world. This claim was intended as the last word: retrospective narratives are and always will be the way we ultimately make sense of things. But this claim, again, requires more than the superiority presupposed in any retrospective narrative. That superiority encompasses the past events that are comprehended within the narrative. But it does not necessarily apply to the future, even if we grant what seems to be the strongest version of Hegel's point: that we will always seek to provide retrospective narratives that can tell us who we are in terms of where we have come from. Even if this is true (as it surely seems to be), there remains the question of whether we want to be what the narrative tells us we are in the future.

Hegel believes that a good retrospective narrative reconciles us to the present, by convincing us that we are beyond the naïve strivings of our earlier selves. But there is a difference between getting "beyond" the past and accepting that the lessons of the past suffice to guide us in the future. In Hegel's own retrospective narrative, which concerns retrospective narration itself, we are supposed to accept that the failures of philosophy's attempts at justification without retrospective narrative have shown us that retrospective narrative is all we need to justify our present and future claims. In the years following Hegel's death, it was this claim that was bitterly attacked. For Marx, the narrative satisfaction provided by Hegel's retrospective account of freedom was a pale substitute for the material satisfaction demanded by the urban poor of the present.[4] For Kierkegaard, the narrative satisfaction of seeing oneself as the product of the past and of one's society was a pale substitute for an authentically lived life.[5] Of these two criticisms, Marx's was the more historically influential, but Kierkegaard's is the more fundamental. Despite Marx's insistence on the priority of material reality over theoretical inquiry, it is clear that his own account of material reality, his

---

[3] The issue of finality and "the end of history" in Hegel is much discussed, often crudely and misleadingly. For a brief and calmer discussion, see Terry Pinkard, *Hegel's Phenomenology: The Sociality of Reason* (Cambridge University Press, 1994), pp. 331–343.

[4] See, for instance, Karl Marx and Friedrich Engels, *The German Ideology*, Part One, ed. C. J. Arthur (International Publishers, 1988), especially pp. 39–57.

[5] Søren Kierkegaard, *Concluding Unscientific Postscript*, trans. David F. Swenson and Walter Lowrie (Princeton University Press, 1988).

own account of the present economic situation, is based on a fully Hegelian retrospective narrative, in which the future of communism is defined by the past failures of capitalism.[6] The reconciliation Hegel sought is projected into the communist future, but this future is already implicit in the analysis of the present. In this sense, Marx's critique of capitalism is as "theoretical" as what he attacks in Hegel. For Kierkegaard, on the other hand, the very idea of a reconciliation to the present is a distasteful affront to the autonomy of the self, which always retains its prerogative to break with the past and set out on its own path. Conformity to the lessons of the past is like conformity to any sort of social practice: a danger to real, individual commitment, which Kierkegaard regards as the criterion for a meaningful life.

The standard Hegelian reply to Kierkegaard is to attack his notion of individual commitment as a naïve return to the abstract notion of freedom (in what sense is Kierkegaard an advance over Kant or even the Stoics?), to point out that this abstract freedom will inevitably be lacking in content (to live meaningfully, does Kierkegaard really need to be a Christian, or can he be essentially anything?), and then to argue that whatever content is chosen can always be folded back into a historical narrative that shows why the individual chose some particular kind of life (was Kierkegaard not like a lot of other Protestants influenced by Romanticism?). All of this is right as far as it goes, but it essentially avoids Kierkegaard's most important point, which is that you can tell the sort of retrospective narrative that Hegel wants us to tell, and still not be reconciled to the present. Kierkegaard did more than defend a notion of radical autonomy; he also linked his defense to a historical narrative in which the modern world and its liberal and democratic tendencies were a greater threat to our autonomy.[7] In different ways, Nietzsche and Freud (and more recently, Foucault) went on to offer historical narratives of just this sort: they each saw the direction of modern social life as endangering our capacities for an autonomous life.[8] The important point for our purposes is not which of these narratives is right, whether any of these specific criticisms of modernity should be accepted. For now the important point is that a retrospective history of our

---

[6] Marx and Engels, *The German Ideology*, Part One, pp. 52–57 and 82–95.

[7] Kierkegaard, *The Present Age*, trans. Alexander Dru (Harper and Row, 1962).

[8] Friedrich Nietzsche, *On the Genealogy of Morals*, trans. Walter Kauffman and R. J. Hollingdale (Vintage, 1989); Sigmund Freud, *Five Lectures on Psychoanalysis*, ed. and trans. James Strachey (Norton, 1977), and *Civilization and its Discontents*, ed. and trans. James Strachey (Norton, 1961); and Michel Foucault, *Discipline and Punish: The Birth of the Prison*, trans. Alan Sheridan (Vintage, 1979), and *The History of Sexuality, Volume I: An Introduction*, trans. Robert Hurley (Vintage, 1980).

freedom and rationality does not necessarily show us to be more free and rational today, even though we cannot "go back" to the naïve perspective of the past (a Hegelian point on which Nietzsche and Freud themselves were especially insistent). A retrospective narrative can show us why we have the commitments we have, and if it is especially compelling, it could even show us why those commitments are in some sense inevitable for us. But this is not yet to show us that these commitments are the right ones. In their own ways, Kierkegaard, Nietzsche, and Freud are all good Hegelians, telling us how we got to be who we are. But they all remind us that admiring ourselves at the end of the story is another matter.

Hegel was right that justification does not proceed in the abstract, and he was right to say that any particular conception of justification can always be supplanted by a historical story that understands it as a naïve perspective that we have now comprehended and gone beyond. He was right that retrospective narrative always claims a special superiority over the perspectives it comprehends. But he was wrong to say that this kind of narrative satisfies our demands for justification. There will always be Hegelian narratives that can place a particular demand for justification in a wider historical context. But the larger Hegelian narrative that tried to place the general demand for justification in its historical context cannot show us that, to count as fully mature, we need to treat retrospective narrative as justification. Even if we are Hegelian subjects, even if we cannot but think of ourselves as maturing, we cannot confuse maturity with improvement.

Further reading

Ameriks, Karl (ed.). *The Cambridge Companion to German Idealism* (Cambridge University Press, 2000).

Avineri, Shlomo. *Hegel's Theory of the Modern State* (Cambridge University Press, 1972).

Beiser, Frederick (ed.). *The Cambridge Companion to Hegel* (Cambridge University Press, 1993).

_____. *Hegel* (Routledge, 2005).

Bencivenga, Ermanno. *Hegel's Dialectical Logic* (Oxford University Press, 2000).

Fackenheim, Emil. *The Religious Dimension in Hegel's Thought* (University of Chicago Press, 1967).

Forster, Michael. *Hegel and Skepticism* (Harvard University Press, 1989).

_____. *Hegel's Idea of a Phenomenology of Spirit* (University of Chicago Press, 1998).

Hardimon, Michael. *Hegel's Social Philosophy: The Project of Reconciliation* (Cambridge University Press, 1994).

Harris, H. L. *Hegel: Phenomenology and System* (Hackett, 1995).

_____. *Hegel's Ladder* (Hackett, 1997).

Houlgate, Stephen. *Freedom, Truth and History: An Introduction to Hegel's Philosophy* (Routledge, 1991).

Hyppolite, Jean. *Genesis and Structure of Hegel's* Phenomenology of Spirit, trans. Samuel Cherniak and John Heckman (Northwestern University Press, 1974).

Kojève, Alexandre. *Introduction to the Reading of Hegel*, trans. James Nichols (Basic Books, 1969).

Lauer, Quentin. *A Reading of Hegel's* Phenomenology of Spirit (Fordham University Press, 1976).

Norman, Richard. *Hegel's Phenomenology: A Philosophical Introduction* (Ashgate, 1991).

Patten, Alan. *Hegel's Idea of Freedom* (Oxford University Press, 1999).

Pinkard, Terry. *Hegel's Phenomenology: The Sociality of Reason* (Cambridge University Press, 1994).

_____. *Hegel: A Biography* (Cambridge University Press, 2000).

_____. *German Philosophy 1760–1860: The Legacy of Idealism* (Cambridge University Press, 2003).

Pippin, Robert. *Hegel's Idealism: The Satisfactions of Self-Consciousness* (Cambridge University Press, 1979).

————. *Modernism as a Philosophical Problem* (Blackwell, 1991).

————. *Idealism as Modernism: Hegelian Variations* (Cambridge University Press, 1997).

Redding, Paul. *Hegel's Hermeneutics* (Cornell University Press, 1996).

Solomon, Robert. *In the Spirit of Hegel* (Oxford University Press, 1983).

Stern, Robert. *Hegel and the* Phenomenology of Spirit (Routledge, 2002).

Stewart, Jon. *The Unity of Hegel's* Phenomenology of Spirit (Northwestern University Press, 2000).

Taylor, Charles. *Hegel* (Cambridge University Press, 1975).

————. *Hegel and Modern Society* (Cambridge University Press, 1979).

Westphal, Kenneth. *Hegel's Epistemology* (Hackett, 2003).

Westphal, Merold. *History and Truth in Hegel's Phenomenology* (Humanities Press, 1978).

Williams, Robert. *Hegel's Ethics of Recognition* (University of California Press, 1998).

Wood, Allen. *Hegel's Ethical Thought* (Cambridge University Press, 1990).

Index